10
SW37

Fame

D0226315

THE ART OF LIVING SERIES
Series Editor: Mark Vernon

From Plato to Bertrand Russell philosophers have engaged wide audiences on matters of life and death. *The Art of Living* series aims to open up philosophy's riches to a wider public once again. Taking its lead from the concerns of the ancient Greek philosophers, the series asks the question "How should we live?". Authors draw on their own personal reflections to write philosophy that seeks to enrich, stimulate and challenge the reader's thoughts about their own life. In a world where people are searching for new insights and sources of meaning, *The Art of Living* series showcases the value of philosophy and reveals it as a great untapped resource for our age.

Published
Clothes   *John Harvey*
Deception   *Ziyad Marar*
Fame   *Mark Rowlands*
Hunger   *Raymond Tallis*
Illness   *Havi Carel*
Pets   *Erica Fudge*
Sport   *Colin McGinn*
Wellbeing   *Mark Vernon*
Work   *Lars Svendsen*

Forthcoming
Death   *Todd May*
Middle Age   *Chris Hamilton*
Sex   *Seiriol Morgan*

Fame

Mark Rowlands

ACUMEN

For Emma

© Mark Rowlands, 2008

This book is copyright under the Berne Convention.
No reproduction without permission.
All rights reserved.

First published in 2008 by Acumen

Acumen Publishing Limited
Stocksfield Hall
Stocksfield
NE43 7TN
www.acumenpublishing.co.uk

ISBN: 978-1-84465-157-3

British Library Cataloguing-in-Publication Data
A catalogue record for this book is available
from the British Library.

Designed and typeset by Kate Williams, Swansea.
Printed and bound by Biddles Ltd, King's Lynn.

Contents

1. Girls gone wild: fame and vfame

Fame gone wild

The things I do in the name of research. It is an idea breathtaking in its brilliance and stunning in its simplicity; if only I had thought of it when I was a teenager. The person who actually thought it up was someone called Joseph R. Francis, currently facing federal prison on tax evasion charges, which goes to show just how much a good idea can screw up your life if it's followed by a not so good idea. The essence of Francis's good idea is this: you ask girls to take their clothes off. Here's the surprising part: they do. *Girls Gone Wild* is an extraordinarily successful series of short films. The title effectively captures the oeuvre. The films feature teenage or twenty-something girls going wild in various, broadly sexual, ways, including exposing breasts and/or buttocks to the camera with additional fondling of said breasts or buttocks if deemed necessary. In hindsight, perhaps my office wasn't the best place to be conducting this research; various quizzical eyebrows have been raised by the odd student who shows up unannounced at my office to ask questions about this or that essay. Leave me alone: can't you see I'm working? Anyway, my hands are tied. There's no way that Mrs Rowlands is going to let me watch this at home.

The question – and this question effectively provides the focus of this book – is: why? Why would anyone want to manhandle – or, more accurately, "girlhandle" – themselves in front of a poten- tial audience of millions? Why anyone would want to watch this is

1

an equally good question, but one for another book, not this one. These are just ordinary girls next door: especially if next door for you is, as it is for me, a beach in Florida. Most "girls gone wild" seem to be on spring break or in some other party-heavy zone. Presumably, convincing their parents that their sky-high college tuition fees are being well spent is not high on their agenda. Nor, it seems, is the acquisition of money for themselves any part of the deal. What they want, it seems, is neither money nor respect but fame. And if so, this says a lot about the current state of fame.

The assumption that *Girls Gone Wild* will provide one with a safe and reliable route to fame is, of course, rather questionable. I've learned this morning that if you've seen one buxom twenty-something fondling themselves, you've seen them all. But one can, I suppose, dare to dream. One day it's *Girls Gone Wild*, the next you're a tramp in a Nickleback video. And from there the world is your reality television oyster. That a dream is wildly implausible need not stop people from dreaming it. Fame, in the early-twenty-first-century West, is the game. This book is about fame, not just fame in the traditional sense, but also a new and peculiar sort of fame that characterizes the turn-of-the-millennium West. In *Girls Gone Wild* we find, I think, the quintessence of this new and peculiar sort of fame.

I am not trying to sound judgemental; still less misogynistic. I have no moral problem with girls who have gone wild. I come not to judge but to understand. And, in particular, I want to understand the sort of fame that motivates them and why it is such a powerful motivation. In any case, men are equally susceptible to the lure of fame. Mercifully, there is, at least as far as I know, no corresponding series "Boys Gone Wild": presumably because there are significantly fewer people interested in watching boys manhandle themselves. Nonetheless, men are keen to get in on the act in any way they can. And to do so they have to find entirely new, and often rather eccentric, ways of publicly humiliating themselves. Thus on a fairly recent (at the time of writing) episode of *The Graham Norton Show*, a small but nonetheless non-negligible portion of the programme was devoted to watching a man have his back, rear and scrotum waxed (the "back, crack and sack", as it is apparently known in the industry). There's no judgement here: perhaps hairless nether regions do indeed have their merits. But who would volunteer to have such regions rendered hairless in front of an audience of millions? Who would want to do it? And, more importantly, why would they want to do it? This rather ghastly image provides, I think, another garish example of modern fame and our obsession with it.

Who wants fame? It seems many of us do. Indeed, judging from the popularity of television shows that deal, in one way or another, with fame – and television is, of course, the most accurate barometer of modern culture – it seems that most of us do. There are programmes whose entire *raison d'être* is to take people off the street and make them famous. Sometimes this trades on modest talents they possess innately. *American Idol* (the US version of *Pop Idol*) is the most popular programme on US television, and Simon Cowell is slightly more powerful than the President. Each new series of this show is preceded by a nationwide series of auditions, attended by tens of thousands of people. These people often camp for days outside the arenas where the auditions are to take place just to make sure they get their chance: shanty towns of huddled masses all united by the belief – usually erroneous – that they can sing. Popular spin-offs and/or variations include shows that turn on people dancing in order to become famous (or because they are already famous but their fame is on the slide), or people showing that they have some or other talent, however stunningly peripheral it may be. (It was satirist Bill Maher in his talk show *Real Time with Bill Maher* who summed up the delicious irony of the denouement of the most recent season of the show *America's Got Talent*: "If your winner is a ventriloquist, then America *hasn't* got talent". Still, any show that has "the Hoff" in it can't be all bad.) Other types of programme eschew the need for talent in any form, *Big Brother* and associated spin-offs providing the most obvious example. (And no, as a matter of fact, you don't watch it because it is an interesting psychological experiment, no matter how much you insist on telling yourself and others this; you watch it because you are a sad loser who has become addicted to the spectacle of human failure and broken dreams every Friday night.) Admittedly, having to trade pleasantries with the worryingly manic host Davina McCall on exiting the house can't be easy. But for the most part, all you have to do to be on *Big Brother* is be willing to sit in a house for what seems to be an eternity (at least to me) and be willing to do slightly more outrageous things than the people did on the previous series. It also seems to help if you are sad or unusual in some way.

Other types of show deal with the lives, loves, tribulations and scandals of those people who are already famous, perhaps because they have already appeared on a show of the former sort. Don't get me started on these. Admittedly, during the months of rigorous and exhaustive research I have had to put into this book watching *E! Entertainment*, I have become rather attached to hosts Ryan Seacrest and Debbie Matenopoulos and Giuliana Rancic (*née* de Pandi) and even Sal Masekela, despite his occasional anti-vegetarian tirades, and their increasingly desperate and persistent attempts to get me interested in their "Daily Ten" entertainment news stories. (On reflection, I have come to realize, I think, that there are actually two shows involved, of which *E! Entertainment* is one and *The Daily Ten* is the other. But since there is absolutely no discernible difference between the two –in terms of form, presentation or content – I am going, on general grounds of Leibniz's identity of indiscernibles, to refuse to distinguish them. Believe me, until you have seen the same story repeated over and over again, with a gushing enthusiasm that suggests it is for the first time, for the best part of an hour, you don't know the meaning of the word "persistence".) I also think Ben Lyons's film reviews are really rather good;

at least, we usually concur on the relative merits of the new releases. However, even the sterling efforts of Ryan, Giuliana, Debbie, Sal and Ben can't paper over the obvious question: how sad would you have to be to actually be interested in this stuff? The thing is, many people *are* interested. We're not talking *American Idol* or *Dancing with the Stars* sorts of figures, but, nonetheless, *E! Entertainment*, along with various other programmes of that ilk, has a significant, solid and above all loyal viewing base. Not only do we want to be famous, many of us are fascinated by those who are famous. And, last but not least, there are the paper versions of these sorts of shows: *Hello* magazine, *OK* magazine, *In Touch*, *National Enquirer* – the list goes on, and all sell in their gazillions.

In short, from humble beginnings, fame has, in the past decade or so, as the twentieth century slid into the twenty-first, risen from relative obscurity like a Joaquin Phoenix from the ashes. Our fascination with it, fascination sometimes bordering on obsession, has become the most pronounced cultural phenomenon of our time. However, as we shall see, in the process, something has happened to fame. Our obsession with fame has transformed it. Perhaps all the attention has gone to its head. But, for one reason or another, fame is not at all what it used to be. *Fame has gone wild.*

Opium of the people

In *The Present Age*, the nineteenth-century Danish philosopher Søren Kierkegaard provides a perceptive and prescient analysis of modern nihilism. He calls nihilism "levelling", and defines this as a situation in which "qualitative distinctions are weakened by a gnawing reflection" (1962: 43). By "qualitative distinction", Kierkegaard means distinctions of perceived *quality* – distinctions between what is thought to be important or worthwhile and what is not:

5

> A disobedient youth is no longer in fear of his schoolmaster
> – the relation is rather one of indifference in which school-
> master and pupil discuss how a good school should be run.
> To go to school no longer means to be in fear of the master,
> or merely to learn, but rather implies being interested in the
> problem of education.   (*Ibid.*: 43)

Admittedly, it probably doesn't help matters when a student shows up at his professor's office only to find him watching *Girls Gone Wild*. But underlying Kierkegaard's worry is not a wistful nostalgia for more socially conservative times. What bothers Kierkegaard about this levelling of distinctions between teachers and students, fathers and sons, kings and subjects, and so on, is that it neither conserves nor destroys. Rather, "it leaves everything standing but cunningly empties it of significance" (*ibid.*: 45). I shall try to show that this, in essence, is what has happened to fame. It has undergone a kind of Kierkegaardian levelling that empties it of significance.

Kierkegaard is very clear that this sort of levelling is not, prima-rily, a social problem. Fundamentally, it is a problem for the indi-vidual, although, admittedly, for the father of modern existentialism pretty much everything was a problem for the individual. The level-ling of qualitative distinctions – distinctions of worth or value – makes it impossible to be truly committed to anything. It may seem strange to think of our age as one characterized by an absence of commitment; this is an age where tens of thousands of people are willing to camp out for days to secure their shot at *Idol* fame. But commitment, for Kierkegaard, is a complex concept that involves not only effort but achievement: commitment is, at the very least, worthwhile effort. And the distinction between effort and achieve-ment – between effort that is and effort that is not worthwhile – is one of the things that is lost in the levelling down of qualitative distinctions.

The problem of commitment is a particularly important one for Kierkegaard because, for him, being committed and being a self or person is ultimately one and the same thing. Kierkegaard, famously, found the solution to his problem in religion and the "leap of faith" that underlies it. And this appeal also has echoes in the case of fame, although for reasons that stem more from Marx than Kierkegaard. Recall Marx's famous dictum that religion "is the opium of the people". Religion can be this way only because it is available to all. All are capable of salvation, irrespective of the accidents of birth and their innate talents and endowments. In the absence of this universal application, religion might be opium, but it would not be for the masses.

For whatever reason, religion just doesn't seem to be cutting it any more as the opium of the people. Why this should be is, I think, genuinely puzzling. It's not that people aren't religious any more. In large swathes of the United States, Christianity is positively *de rigeur*. And even in the godless United Kingdom, over 70 per cent of the population call themselves Christian. And the rest of the country seems to comprise Muslims and Hindus and Jedi Knights (if the last UK census is anything to go by). If it's not the numbers, then maybe it's the degree of conviction? Maybe the majority still profess to believe in the opiate powers of eternal salvation but they're not quite as sure as they used to be: certainty has been replaced with wishing. Or maybe it's just that the opium offered is, in today's culture of instant satisfaction, just a little too delayed. Who knows? But for whatever reason, in our present age, rather than Kierkegaard's, the role of universal opiate has been taken over, to a considerable extent, by fame. And for this to occur, fame had to undergo a certain kind of "levelling" that made it universal: available in principle to everyone, irrespective of accidents of birth and innate endowments. In short, fame is where it is today because it became more like religion used to be.

R-E-S-P-E-C-T

One way of understanding the levelling undergone by fame is by seeing it in terms, fundamentally, of a breaking of the connection between fame and respect. Fame has recently changed the company it keeps. At one time, fame was closely associated with respect; and not just respect but deserved respect. But recently they have gone their separate ways. Fame was never the same thing as respect – they are two different concepts – but they used to be strongly associated. But, much like Britney Spears and Kevin Federline, there has been a pronounced parting of the ways.

Let's look first at the concept of respect. Suppose you have a job. You work hard in that job, and as a result become very good at it. Your achievements are notable and, consequently, your colleagues come to respect you. Of course, human nature being what it is, it may well be a grudging respect; they may also be jealous. But they have no choice: your achievements are there for all to see. You have forced them to give you their respect. The life of an ambitious employee may well be, to a considerable extent, a life motivated by the quest for respect.

Why do we do it? Why is respect so important? Well, one reason is, presumably, the money. Your employer likes you when you are respected and is more inclined to throw money at you because of it. In part, they have to. Other potential employers – who have come to realize that you are a person to be respected – are likely to attempt to head hunt you by throwing even more money at you. If you play your cards right, you can be raking in the money in no time at all. But is money the whole story? I doubt it.

Suppose you had managed to talk your way into a highly paid job, a position whose financial rewards were entirely unrelated to your actual achievements, which were mediocre. Your colleagues openly ridicule you. Perhaps this is because they are jealous of your immense salary. But nonetheless, the ridicule rings true: both you and they know that you are not very good at your job and you don't deserve the salary you are being paid. The money is, of course, a consolation: there's no denying that. You could think: who cares? – I can buy and sell them several times over. But if you had the choice you would probably admit that you would like the respect too. And if you don't, then that might well be because you have become the sort of person for whom the only measure of respect is money. Such a person is not unheard of, but even today is surprisingly uncommon. Unless you're very lucky, to earn money you have to become immersed into a certain discipline – intellectual, financial, athletic and so on – and this discipline has its own standards of excellence. And to become really good – and so respected – in that discipline, you genuinely have to buy into those standards. Someone who treats their discipline, and its associated standards, as merely a game, the sole purpose of which is to garner financial rewards, is not likely to do very well in their discipline. The con always works best when you believe the con. We might want both respect and money. But, in general, the value of respect does not simply reduce to the value of money. Typically, respect has a value that is separate from and additional to the value of money. This is not to say that the value of respect is greater than the value of money. Rather, the claim is that the value we attach to respect is not the same thing as the value we attach to money.

The value we attach to respect also does not reduce to the value we attach to achievement. Suppose your achievements in whatever career you have chosen are, due to the slings and arrows of outrageous fortune, overlooked, even though they are, by any reasonable and objective standards, praiseworthy. You might try to reconcile yourself to this outrage by saying: screw the money – the work is its own reward. By this, you don't have in mind any vaguely protestant idea that hard work is inherently ennobling. Rather, the idea is that there are certain things you can control in life and certain things you can't. The quality of the work you produce in whatever discipline you work is something over which, within the limits set by your own innate talents and abilities, you have control. Other people's reactions to your work are something over which you have no or little control. You have produced a masterpiece of da Vincian proportions. So what if no one recognizes it for what it is worth? You know what you have done even if no one else does; and when you look yourself in the eye in the mirror each day, you can feel satisfied with this.

However, this attempt to reconcile yourself with your unfortunate destiny doesn't really ring true either. Knowledge – your self-knowledge – of your achievements, if that is what they indeed are and you are not simply deceiving yourself about their merits, is undoubted consolation. But, all things being equal, wouldn't you really rather have your achievements plus recognition of them? In the circumstances, a little bit of respect doesn't seem too much to ask, really. It is merely what you deserve. You believe that you have produced a masterpiece. And let's suppose your belief is, in fact, true. Nonetheless, the greatness of your work is something that is going to be recognized only long after you are gone. During your lifetime, your work is going to be ridiculed. It would be impossibly demanding for you to laugh off the widespread derision your work receives before you have shuffled off this mortal coil. That achievement is its own reward, and what is important is to be able to look yourself in the eye in the mirror, is what people say when they're dead inside.

Financial reward for your achievements is a form of recognition. However, the value of fame does not seem to reduce to this sort of recognition. The opposite reaction is to shun the need for recognition, and simply focus on your achievements, whether lauded or not. However, respect has a value over and above the value of your achievements. So, the conclusion that seems to be forced on us is that respect involves appropriate recognition of your achievements, where this recognition does not reduce to the merely financial (although that, undoubtedly, helps).

The distinction between the value of an achievement and the value of the recognition of that achievement means that we have to distinguish two senses of the word "respect". The word has both a descriptive and a normative sense. We can speak not only of who *is*, in fact, respected; we can speak also of who *should be* respected. We use the word respect descriptively when we use it to describe who, as a matter of fact, is respected. We use the word normatively when we use it to make claims about who should be respected. To see the difference, consider this claim:

Paris Hilton is more respected than Nelson Mandela.

Who knows: in certain sections of the population, this claim might actually be true – although I hope not. At least, it might be true when the word "respect" is used descriptively. For when it is used like this, whether or not the claim is true depends only on how many people respect Hilton versus how many people respect Mandela (and on how much respect each person allots to their preferred icon). However, when the word "respect" is used normatively, it pertains not to how things actually are, but to how they should, or ought to, be. Understood normatively, the claim would be that Hilton is more worthy of respect than Mandela. And, whatever the charms of Ms Hilton, it would be difficult to make a case for this claim being true.

For the purposes of this book, and for understanding what has happened to the idea of fame, it is the normative sense of respect that is important. Respect, in this normative sense, amounts to the idea of being worthy of respect. Alternatively, we might distinguish between "respect" and "respectable", where this latter term connotes the idea that the respect must not simply be given but also deserved. Normatively, respect is deserved respect. For example, if you have, in fact, produced a masterpiece of da Vincian proportions, and are not merely deceiving yourself about this, then other people ought to or should treat you in a certain manner: a manner that evinces recognition of your achievement. If they don't, then something has gone wrong. A wrong has been done, and that wrong has been done to you. In this way, the normative concept of respect is bound up with ideas of right and wrong. The concept is bound up with ideas of what you deserve, or what is your due and how other people ought to or should treat you.

It is not clear whether the idea of fame is ambiguous in a way similar to that of respect. Consider the claim:

Paris Hilton is more famous than Nelson Mandela.

Understood descriptively, the truth of this claim is simply a matter of how many people have heard of Hilton and how many have heard of Mandela; if more have heard of Hilton then the claim is true. In this descriptive sense of fame, the numbers are everything. And in certain sections of the population, I suspect, this claim is almost certainly true.

However, one might also want to claim that there is a normative sense of the concept of fame. Actually, I'm not sure that there is. The descriptive sense of the idea of fame is, I think, far more dominant than the descriptive sense of the idea of respect. One manifestation of this is that there is no corresponding form of the distinction between respect and respectable: that is, there is no corresponding distinction between "fame" and "fameable". However, I can see why someone might want to claim that there is a normative sense of fame. The idea is, no doubt, occasioned by the sense of ruefulness that accompanies contemplation of the above sentence and the realization that it might, in fact, be true. What is the world coming to, one might think, that things could be so? In addition to the descriptive sense of fame, therefore, we might want to add the notion of deserved fame.

For the purposes of this book, and understanding what has happened to the idea of fame, it is the normative sense of respect that is most relevant and the descriptive sense of fame. The two used to be closely connected in this sense: fame, in the descriptive sense, used to track respect, in the normative sense. That is, fame used to track deserved respect. By "track" all I mean is a reliable – although not perfect – correlation. Fame, in the descriptive sense, used to be correlated, in a reasonably reliable way, with deserved respect. The correlation was far from perfect, and mistakes were often made. In no age has the property of being a talentless hack necessarily excluded the property of being famous. Nonetheless, until recently, fame and deserved respect used to co-occur together in reasonably reliable way.

"Respect" in this context means roughly "special or distinctive respect". Presumably all human beings are worthy of respect, in virtue of being sentient creatures who can suffer or enjoy life and the events and experiences it contains. As such, all human beings should be treated with the respect that goes with being such creatures: for being, as it is sometimes called, *subjects-of-a-life*. The same, I would argue, is true of many other creatures. But when I talk of respect and its connection to fame, I am, of course, not talking about this general sort of respect that any human being is due. Rather, I am talking about a special or distinctive sort of respect that goes with having achieved something noteworthy, or having some talent that is in some way exceptional. And this, by definition, only some people can have. It is this specific sort of respect that fame, in its traditional sense, tended to track. Any person, it goes without saying, no matter how unremarkable or untalented should be accorded the respect that goes with being a sentient creature that has feelings and experiences: they are worthy of that sort of respect, and what makes them worthy is the fact that they are sentient. But they have done nothing to earn the special or distinctive sort of respect that goes with excellence or achieve-ment. Henceforth, my use of the word "respect" should be taken, unless specified otherwise, as referring to this special or distinctive form of respect.

The correlation between fame and this special or distinctive sort of respect has now begun to break down. There are two ways in which this is so, one more important than the other. Indeed, one of the ways is, I think, a symptom of the other. To understand what I mean, we should distinguish between (i) who is becoming famous, and (ii) the type of fame these people have. The thesis is that the type of fame people possess today is quite different from the type of fame they used to possess. One result of this is that different people are becoming famous today: the sort of people who wouldn't, in general, have had a snowball's chance in hell of becoming famous in days gone by. But this is just a symptom of the transformation in our concept of fame.

The most obvious, but least important, manifestation of the breakdown is the number of singularly untalented people who are currently famous. What, to take just one of many obvious examples, has Chantelle Houghton done to become famous? Chantelle was the ringer on a UK series of *Celebrity Big Brother*: the non-celebrity who was put into the show to see if she could pass herself off to her celebrity housemates as a fellow celebrity. She did, and fame, in the form of television shows and reasonably lucrative book contracts, followed quickly on the show's heels. Indeed, major publishing houses who once specialized in books with quirky topics such as – I don't know, off the top of my head – introductions to philosophy through blockbuster science-fiction movies, or gripping accounts of central issues in moral and political philosophy through the medium of highly successful television shows, now only want to deal with Chantelle, glamour model Jordan and *Big Brother* housemate Jade.

Or, rather, wanted to. This new sort of fame – undeserved fame, if we want to use the normative version of the concept – is notoriously ephemeral. Jordan – who used the television show *I'm a Celebrity Get Me Out of Here* to propel herself further into the limelight – is still, apparently, doing more than OK famewise, and even recently tried to conquer the United States – although no one really noticed. Jade Goody – who used *Big Brother* to the same effect – is fading fast. And hardly anyone remembers Chantelle. The fickleness of this sort of fame is easy to understand. Fame of this sort can be granted at whim, but without any attachment to any form of virtue or excellence – anything that would make its subject worthy of respect – it can be just as easily withdrawn; and it usually is. Since this new sort of fame is not grounded in enduring features of a person – features such as virtue, excellence or achievement – then there is no reason why it should attach to a person in any enduring way. Rather, this new form of fame seems driven largely by boredom – the ennui characteristic of a society that has become so comfortable that it is starting to feel uncomfortable about itself – and is attracted to the shiny baubles of the new and unfamiliar.

What is much more important – and what I am going to be talking about in this book – is not who becomes famous under the new regime, but what has happened to fame in the process. It is the type of fame that is of primary importance, and not who has it. Indeed, who has it is merely a symptom of the transformation in our concept of fame. Fame used to attach to people in virtue of the properties that made them worthy of respect. Now, however, there has come into existence a form of fame that does not attach to people in virtue of those properties, and indeed has nothing to do with those properties whatsoever. Even people who *are* famous in virtue of properties that make them worthy of respect also have this new sort of fame. This is, perhaps, the most insidious way in which this new form of fame acts: it attaches to people who are already famous – and justifiably so. But it attaches to them not because of the properties or features that have made them, justifiably, famous but for other reasons altogether. This may sound cryptic. It almost certainly sounds confusing. In the next section I'll explain exactly what I mean.

Bend it like Beckham

In days of yore, people became famous when and because they had accomplished something that made them worthy of respect, or because they had some exceptional talent that made them worthy of respect. This is what I mean by saying that the descriptive sense of fame tracked the normative sense of respect. For example, Stanley Matthews was a famous footballer (in the sense employed outside North America). Why? He was before my time, of course, but by all accounts he was rather good at it. His fame stemmed from his ability and associated merit. He was famous because of his ability and resulting achievements; whatever fame attached to him attached to him in virtue of this ability and these achievements. Of Matthews the man, we know very little. We know even less of Emile Puskas, Jon Charles or the sublime Eusébio. Fame did not come to attach itself to Matthews, or any of these others, because of anything other than his ability and achievements.

Did, perchance, Matthews have sex with the bisexual press liaison worker/translator assigned to him? The very same press liaison worker who was once seen on a reality television show interfering with a pig: an entirely different way, apparently, in which a girl might go wild. This is, to say the least, unlikely. To begin with, who was going to assign Matthews a press liaison officer? He was a footballer not a celebrity. I'm not even sure press liaison workers had been invented yet. Moreover, in Matthews's day, reality television shows definitely hadn't been invented. And even if they had, porcine interfering activities probably wouldn't have figured prominently in them.

So, what of Stanley Matthews the man? What did he do? We just don't know. We might be able to find out, if we were to ask his friends, assuming they are still alive and willing to tell a tale. But we won't find out by trawling through the archives of the *Sun* or the *National Enquirer* tabloids, or, for that matter, any tabloid or proto-tabloid that happened to be around in Matthews's day. What went on in Matthews's private life stayed in Matthews's private life. We know him through, and because of, how good he was on the football field.

Let's contrast this with the life and times of David Beckham. I speak as someone who did their undergraduate degree in Manchester, and who indeed, for a year, lived merely a stone's throw from Old Trafford, the stadium that is home to Manchester United: I speak as someone who is, therefore, an honorary Manc (Mancunian) – or at least so I would argue when United are doing well, which, let's face it, is most of the time. And speaking as an arguably honorary Manc, I would have to say that Becks was a decent, nay good, footballer. At his peak, when he could still run, he might even have been very good. In his early twenties, he could play in several positions. As he got older, his abilities coalesced into performing a very creditable role on the right side of midfield; from his mid-twenties his abilities began to decline considerably the further he was moved from there. Defensive grunt was never really one of his fortes. He was a gifted taker of free kicks just outside the box and, at his height, his abilities in this regard were surpassed by no one. But was he the best footballer in the world? Definitely not. Was he the best footballer in England? Probably not. Was he the best footballer on the Manchester United team? Almost certainly not: most people agree that Ryan Giggs and Roy Keane were superior, and many would want to make a case out for Eric Cantona, despite his failures in Europe.

So why is it that Becks now commands $50 million a year with LA Galaxy? Doesn't it seem a little odd that Becks is on $50 million a year for, apparently, doing very little, and his more talented ex-team mates have to either (i) still try to drag their ageing bodies around Old Trafford each Saturday afternoon or, worse (ii) manage Sunderland.

The answer is, of course, merchandising. That's why Real Madrid wanted Beckham too before the Galaxy. Becks can sell so many things for you: most notably soccer shirts that read "10 Beckham" on the back. In the newly affluent Far East, they love those shirts. And then there are the posters, and the more general image rights now controlled by the Galaxy. Stanley Matthews wouldn't have a clue what you were talking about. But more generally: why Becks? Why not the more talented team mates, Giggs and Keane? What has China got against them?

You might think that the answer lies in the fact that Becks has seemed to court publicity in a way that Giggs and Keane never did. This may be true, but when has this ever mattered? If you ask him questions about his private life, Keane is likely to tell you, in his best Mayfield accent, to "Feck off!" But when has this ever stopped the determined and organized tabloid warriors? To them, that's like a red rag to a bull. When Keane was sent home from the 2002 World Cup – having told the then Republic of Ireland manager Mick McCarthy to "Feck off" (among other things) – the paparazzi descended on his house like a biblical plague of locusts. His wife had been holed up in the house for days. When Roy arrived back, in what was surely one of the greatest and defining moments of his life, he told them all to "Feck off", and took his labrador for a walk. My point is that this is not going to discourage the tabloid army. You can tell them all to "Feck off" all you like, but they're going to decide who is and who isn't going to. If you doubt this, just ask Britney Spears.

It can't hurt, of course, that Becks married well. But that simply raises the further question: why her? Many people claim that Posh can't sing. Personally, I think that might be a little harsh. But, let's face it, she's no Billie Holiday. She's not even a Christina Aguilera. And her attempts to carve out a solo career since the demise of the Spice Girls, and in particular the stunningly ill-advised attempt to branch out into hip-hop under the tutelage of Damon Dash, have met with either indifference or derision. Yet, her fame has scarcely dimmed since her Spice days. So appealing to Posh to explain the fame of her husband Becks seems to merely invite the further question: why is she so famous?

At this point, some people might be tempted to cite the X-factor, by which they mean not the television show/Simon Cowell vehicle but a certain indefinable *je ne sais quoi* that Posh and Becks have but Giggs and Keane lack. Of course, appealing to the X-factor can scarcely be thought of as an explanation of the success of Posh and Becks. It's more like an admission that we have no idea what the explanation is. It is reminiscent of the explanatory strategy ridiculed by Voltaire in *Candide*: the strategy that tries to explain why opium puts people to sleep by claiming that it has a dormitive virtue. To say that something has a dormitive virtue means that it has a tendency to put people to sleep. So the claim that opium puts people to sleep because it has a dormitive virtue means nothing more than it puts people to sleep because it has a tendency to put people to sleep. And this is not an explanation: it's an admission that you have no idea what the explanation is. Similarly, since all the "X-factor" really means is that one has been stunningly successful, to appeal to the X-factor to explain the success of Posh and Becks is more or less a way of saying that Posh and Becks have been so stunningly successful because they have been so stunningly successful.

Nevertheless, despite its explanatory vacuity, appeal to the X-factor is not necessarily incorrect even if it's not an explanation: it might point us in the general direction of an explanation. Simply sticking with, "it has a dormitive virtue" does not get us very far in understanding the effects of opium. But if we then go on and identify the relevant molecular properties of opium and their effect on the human brain – the properties in virtue of which it has this dormitive virtue – then we would have the explanation we were looking for. What we need to do to understand the X-factor is understand the properties in virtue of which someone has it. That is what this book, in effect, is about.

The X-factor is, I think, widely misunderstood. It's usually presented as a claim about something that people like Posh and Becks have that we don't recognize or understand. But it isn't really like that at all – at least, that is what I am going to argue. The X-factor is not something that Posh and Becks have. It is something that we – the great unwashed masses – lack. And corresponding to this lack is an entirely new type of fame. Stanley Matthews was famous, and justifiably so. He was famous because of his footballing ability. David Beckham is also famous, and, in part, justifiably so. He is famous, in part, because of his footballing ability. But David Beckham's fame has far outstripped, and grown out of all proportion to, this ability. David Beckham is not just famous; he is also what I am going to call "new variant famous". New variant fame – *vfame* – is the distinctive form that fame has taken in the millennial West.

So, in the interests of precision, in the rest of this book I am going to use the following terminology. I shall say that David Beckham is famous in virtue of his footballing ability: that nexus of skills, physical and psychological, that made him a world class footballer. But Becks's vfame does not attach to him in virtue of his footballing ability. It attaches to him in virtue of something else: something, I shall argue, that we lack not that Becks has. Matthews, on the other hand, was just famous. He couldn't have been vfamous: it hadn't been invented yet.

Today, some people, like Beckham, are both famous and vfamous. Some people, like Chantelle, are only vfamous. People have been famous for a long time. But only now is vfame starting to become such a pronounced feature of the cultural landscape: vfame is the distinctive sort of fame that characterizes our times.

The judgement of Paris

I remember exactly where I was when I heard the news. I expect most of us do. America had ground to a standstill, and the spectre of human calamity had forced its way into our living rooms, jarring us out of our quotidian existence and bringing us face to face with the abyss. Who can forget the tears, the recriminations: and more than anything, the numbing sense of disbelief? I refer of course to the tragic "en-vehicling" of Paris Hilton as she made her way back to the LA County Jail – during what was, almost certainly, the long dark lunchtime of her soul. Perhaps you thought I was talking about something else. She wept, she hugged her family; she expressed her disbelief and outrage. And she actually had a point. With the California jail system on the point of collapse through overcrowding, she almost certainly wouldn't have done the time she had to do if she hadn't have been Paris Hilton. The most likely scenario would have seen her released immediately after surrender and processing. Maybe she would have done a couple of days; at the outside a week. But not the truly massive twenty-two days she in fact did.

For those of you not familiar with the details, here they are. As a result of a number of vehicular infractions, involving driving under the influence, recklessness and driving while on a suspended licence, Paris Hilton managed to get herself sentenced to do time in Los Angeles' Lynwood County Jail. She had been admitted to Lynwood two days previously. But then she managed to have herself sprung, citing a mysterious "medical condition". This "condition" ultimately turned out to consist in the fact that, all things considered, she really didn't like being in jail, because she found it a little confining. Swayed by this, the LA County Sheriff released her to serve the rest of her time under house arrest. The judge who sent her to jail, however, (i) apparently didn't like Hilton at all (and her constant flouting of his previous court orders might possibly had something to do with that), and (ii) was apparently enjoying his fifteen minutes of fame (the members of his country club allegedly gave him a standing ovation when he showed up for dinner that night). He immediately ordered her back to jail to serve her "full" term, which, in the LA county penal system, actually amounts to half of the full term. I think Rod Liddle accurately summed up the situation in his commentary of 10 June 2007 in *The Sunday Times* newspaper: "given a longer than usual prison sentence because she's a famous slapper, let out earlier than usual because she's a famous slapper, rearrested and banged up again because she's a famous slapper".

The epithet "slapper", of course, alludes to the way in which Hilton achieved her fame in the first place through the appearance on the internet of a video of her having sex with her then boyfriend, Rick Salomon. Salomon later decided, correctly, that there was more wealth to be accrued from online poker than from public copulation with society girls. And, at the time of writing, Salomon was last seen apparently getting married to Pamela Anderson, who, coincidentally, was herself no stranger to sex tapes leaked to the internet. No one is suggesting, of course, that Hilton was responsible for this leak, but she certainly benefited from it. Reality television fame quickly followed on its heels. It's not like she needed the money, of course: Hilton is the heir to the Hilton hotel dynasty, and worth gazillions. But it seems she wanted more than money; she also wanted fame. And this she certainly achieved. Indeed, her desire for fame has, reportedly, cost her most of her money. Recent reports suggest that she has been disowned, and more importantly, largely disinherited by the Hilton patriarch because of the embarrassment caused him by the sex tape.

Thus, Paris's return to the loving arms of the LA County penal system received blanket coverage in all the mainstream US media, and some decidedly non-mainstream outlets too. The event has become known in popular folklore as the "en-vehicling" of Paris, centering, as it does, on the event of her stepping into the LA County Sheriff's car on her way back to prison. Of course, the comprehensive coverage of this event met with much agonized hand wringing on the part of the very networks that devoted an entire day to covering it. As one CNN news anchor put it: "Are we just so pathetic and so lonely that we have to live through people like Paris Hilton?" And as Jon Stewart, host of the *Daily Show*, replied: "If by 'we' you mean 'CNN', and if by 'lonely' you mean 'nobody's watching us', then 'Yes'!" As Stewart also noted, the chaotic fervour with which the networks, the paparazzi, and almost certainly large numbers of interested bystanders, pursued Paris on that day made the event reminiscent of celebrations of the Cult of the Madonna, associated with the Philippines and other places. Stewart draws the only possible conclusion: either US culture is irrevocably crippled or Paris Hilton is a virgin worthy of worship. Which, of course, brings us back to the Rick Salomon video.

The remarkable interest in the "en-vehicling" of Paris provides a graphic illustration of a decisive break that has taken place in recent years. The fame of Ms Hilton is a new, and inherently strange, form of fame: vfame. Indeed, in Paris Hilton we find a peculiarly pure form of vfame. Hilton achieved fame by being seen on the internet copulating with her then boyfriend. Admittedly, she was famous in society circles before that. But it was the Rick Salomon gig that really brought her to the attention of the sweaty-palmed masses. And since then she is famous for little – or arguably nothing – more than being famous. This is vfame: fame unconnected with any notable form of excellence or achievement. This is not to demean Hilton; I have never met her; and for all I know she might be a lovely person. But there are lots of lovely people out there, most of whom are not famous. Being a lovely person is not, typically, a fame-imbuing characteristic.

It all goes back to Rick Salomon

It is instructive to compare Paris Hilton with someone who really did bring America to a standstill: Osama bin Laden. Undoubtedly one of the most evil and monstrous men in history, he is nevertheless very good at what he does. And this is what he is famous for. Of the man, very little is known. His fame is pure fame. This in itself should ward off the temptation to think that fame is necessarily good while vfame is bad: to the best of my knowledge Hilton isn't a psychopathic mass murderer. Both fame and vfame are, in themselves, morally neutral. It all depends on what you are famous – or vfamous – for.

The fame of Paris Hilton, on the other hand, is pure vfame: she is famous not for what she has done but simply because she is famous. She might, of course, dispute this claim. On her release from jail, she appeared on CNN's *Larry King Live*, where, among other things, she tries to dispel certain widespread misconceptions about her.

King: What's the biggest misconception about you?
Hilton: Well, a misconception that I always hear is that Paris doesn't work for a living. She just, you know, gets money from her family. And I completely disagree with that. I've been earning on my own, by myself. I've not taken any money from my family. I work very hard. I run a business. I had a book on the *New York Times* bestseller list. I'm on my TV show. Did an album. Do movies.

This is all true, but overlooks one fairly obvious point. These activities all stem from, and are made possible by, her vfame. An important part of her business is being paid vast sums of money to show up at nightclubs. One recent movie, *House of Wax*, advertised itself with the slogan: "See Paris Die!" Perhaps *The Hottie and Nottie* will involve a more sympathetic portrayal. I admit, I have not read Paris's book (but am immensely looking forward to doing so), but we shall have cause to revisit some of her literary efforts later: epistles penned from her eight by twelve cell in Lynwood. Without wishing to be unkind, these will, I believe, cast a certain amount of doubt on the idea that her bestseller was such purely on literary merit. Of course, I could be wrong. It is difficult to believe that without the sex tape her television show would have made her as vfamous as she is. And while her singing voice is indeed not unpleasant, it is otherwise unremarkable.

In short: Rick Salomon. It all goes back to Rick Salomon. Whether by accident or design, Ms Hilton identified the surest route to vfame. First of all, you have to be vaguely known already. That's where the girls of *Girls Gone Wild* went wrong: they didn't put in the necessary groundwork. Ms Hilton had achieved a modest level of notoriety as an "It" girl. If you moved in certain circles, you would have known exactly who she was. But the career of an It girl is notoriously ephemeral. Does anyone remember Normandie Keith? So, then, when some people have vaguely heard of you, you have to leak a sex tape to the internet. I can't emphasize enough how important this second part is. This got me thinking. I've written a few books. Some of them actually did quite well. In certain circles at least, some people have vaguely heard of me. So, why not go for it? I did broach the subject with Mrs Rowlands, but unfortunately she's not really up for it. So, I'm afraid it's a life of toiling in obscurity for me.

Given the way she initially achieved it, it is perhaps ironic to describe Paris Hilton as embodying a particularly pure form of vfame. But nonetheless, that is what she does. Vfame is fame unconnected to any achievement or excellence in any recognized form. Vfame does not allow itself to be inconvenienced by these things.

To call this version of fame "new variant fame" – "vfame" – is, of course, an allusion to new variant Creutzfeldt-Jakob disease: vCJD. As everyone knows, CJD is a corrosive and progressive disease of the brain that produces, in its victims, severe dementia followed by death. It's as nasty a way to go as it is possible to imagine. However, traditional CJD had at least one redeeming virtue: it only afflicted the very old. Traditional CJD was, therefore, closely associated with a certain sort of achievement: living to a ripe old age. With vCJD this association is broken. The rogue prion responsible for vCJD is no respecter of age or any other achievements. The only requirement is that you somehow ingest the relevant prion from something – or someone – that already has it: beef from the United Kingdom being the most obvious candidate.

If this analogy is to be anything more than superficial, then there should exist the functional equivalent of a rogue prion: a rogue cultural prion that breaks the connection between fame and achievement, and thus converts traditional fame into vfame. What is this cultural prion? The analogue of the prion, I am going to argue, is to be found in a remarkable philosophical experiment that began in late-seventeenth-century France and continues to this day. This experiment became known as the Enlightenment, and it has made us the people we are today. Some people think of the Enlightenment as an attempt to rewrite history and remake culture as if the preceding two thousand years had never happened. I shall try to convince you that it is anything but that. However, the Enlightenment does have a degenerate form and in this form it is precisely an attempt to ignore the lessons of history. There is nothing wrong with the Enlightenment itself: it was bold and it was brilliant, and it has produced, with the possible exception of fourth century BCE Athens, the greatest civilizations the world has ever seen. Nevertheless, there is a flaw, a crucial instability, that lies at the heart of this project. As a result the project, in addition to its dazzling achievements, also naturally degenerates into something quite different. In this sense, the Enlightenment also has a dark side. It is here that we need to look if we are to understand vfame.

2. Footnotes to Plato

The significance of vfame: an overview

This book is a wide-ranging discussion of the significance of vfame. It is wide ranging in the sense that it runs all the way from a dispute that began in ancient Athens, through certain ideas that originated in seventeenth- and eighteenth-century France, to the rise of religious fundamentalism in the late-twentieth century. Much of the time it might be difficult to see what any of this has to do with either fame or vfame. So, in this section, I want to lay out the argument that I'm going to develop in the rest of the book.

Here is the central idea: vfame is a *symptom*. That is the significance of vfame. The importance of vfame lies not in what it is in itself, but in the fact that it is a symptom of something else. There is nothing morally objectionable about vfame *in itself*. As we have seen, perfectly decent people – as I'm sure Paris Hilton is – can be purely vfamous; and psychopathic mass murderers can be purely famous. Nonetheless, there is something morally questionable about vfame. But this can only be seen when we understand vfame as a symptom of something else.

The question, then, is this: what is vfame a symptom of? I don't want to give away too many of the details at this stage – and, at this stage, they wouldn't make much sense anyway – but, roughly, I am going to argue that vfame is a symptom of a form of cultural degeneration that has a specific character.

This leads to the second question: what sort of cultural degeneration are we talking about? To understand this, we have to examine
the nature of the culture in which the degeneration occurs. Our
culture, I shall try to show, is built on two major principles: the
first, it acquired from ancient Athens, and, in particular, from the
philosopher Plato; the second is more recent, being supplied by
certain intellectual developments that occurred in seventeenth- and
eighteenth-century France. The intellectual heart of the modern
West, I shall argue, is provided by the combination of these ideas.

This leads us to our third question: why should a culture formed
on the basis of these ideas naturally undergo a form of cultural
degeneration? The reason is twofold. First of all, the idea supplied
by Plato and the idea supplied by eighteenth-century France, are
mutually compatible, but only just. They exist in a constant state
of tension with each other. What we call the West always was a
delicate juggling act. Secondly, and more importantly, each of the
ideas naturally degenerates – largely owing to certain deficiencies in
human character – into something else: they naturally deteriorate
into degenerate and pernicious forms. If you think of the West as a
juggling act – as the tension between its two core ideas requires us
to do – then the difficulty facing the juggler is significantly – and
perhaps even fatally – exacerbated by the fact that the balls can, at
any time, turn into shit.

The rest of the book tries to fill in the details of this argument.
We'll get to those in due course. But let's take a quick look at the
ultimate conclusion: the destination of this book. Because of the
sort of intellectual and cultural degeneration I am going to describe,
the world of the early-twenty-first century West can be quickly and
unequivocally characterized. What is distinctive of Western society
of today is the constitutional – and by now we might even legitimately describe it as congenital – inability to distinguish *quality*
from *bullshit*. This is the predicament in which we find ourselves
today. And that, fundamentally, is the significance of vfame.

Fame, vfame and objectivity

As we have seen, traditionally, fame in the descriptive sense tracks respect in the normative sense. That is, traditionally, one became famous by doing or achieving something worthy of respect. More generally, to be famous, in the traditional sense, you generally had to be unusually good at something. And this meant that there were independent and objective standards of competence that you had to meet. Typically, these standards would be discipline-specific: what makes you a good footballer is quite different from what makes you a good Prime Minister, for example. However, the standards are objective and independent of your and others' beliefs, desires and other attitudes in this sense: you can't, in general, be good at something just by deciding or believing that you are – no matter how fervently you might believe it. What made Stanley Matthews worthy of respect – at least on the football field – was that he met and exceeded the normal standards of excellence applied to a professional footballer. It doesn't really matter whether he believed he met or exceeded those standards: it is whether he actually did meet or exceed them that is crucial.

Moreover, excellence in a given discipline or domain is not even essentially a matter of other people's beliefs: what they think of you or your performance. People make mistakes. Even if everybody thinks you are outstanding at something, this doesn't automatically mean that you are: they might be deluded; you might be conning them, and so on (at least, then, you would at least be a good con – it's just that you wouldn't be good at what people think you're good at). In other words, you are overrated. If so, the chances are that whatever fame you accrue through delusion or deception will quickly fade as you are "found out". Traditional fame is tied to excellence and resulting achievement in this sense: traditional fame tracks worthiness of respect; and there are objective and independent standards for being worthy of respect.

It is characteristic of vfame that these objective and independent standards of worthiness or excellence have largely been abandoned. This is true whether vfame attaches to someone with no talents whatsoever, or whether it attaches to someone with definite talents – such as David Beckham – but that attaches to them as something over and above the fame that they justifiably possess. There are no objective and independent standards of excellence that one must satisfy in order to be vfamous – whether one becomes vfamous is largely a matter of luck or timing. Of course, someone's path to vfame might be facilitated by some very intelligent decisions on their part, decisions pertaining to the mood of the public (e.g. is now really a good time to release my sex tape to the internet?). But how you become vfamous is one thing; the standards you have to meet to become vfamous are quite another. In becoming vfamous, you might employ a level of intelligence or processes of reasoning that meet objective and independent standards of excellence. But it is still true that your vfame itself – as opposed to how you achieve it – does not require the satisfaction of any such standards. You might have to be very intelligent – objectively intelligent – in getting people to hear of you, to idolize you, to want to be you. But it does not follow from this that they should have heard of you, idolize you, or want to be you.

One advantage of understanding the distinction between fame and vfame in this way is that it connects up the distinction, in what I shall argue is a useful and illuminating way, with a long and respectable philosophical debate, one that stretches back at least as far as the ancient Greek philosophers, Socrates and Plato. In its essence, the debate is between what are known as *relativism* and *objectivism*. These two concepts, I am going to argue, have played an enormous role in shaping the current contours of our civilization. Accordingly, some of the greatest minds that ever lived have been employed in thinking about these concepts, refining, sharpening and elaborating them. As a result, these ideas are not as unambiguous as they once were. Indeed, they now mean different things to different people. What I am going to do in this chapter is take these ideas back to their historical and intellectual roots.

"Man is the measure of all things"

Alfred North Whitehead was a very good philosopher of the early twentieth century. Due to the vicissitudes of fortune (or rather fame), today it's generally only professional philosophers who have heard of him. And if anyone outside the ivory tower knows anything about him at all, it is probably because of something he said about the ancient Greek philosopher, Plato. Whitehead claimed that the "safest general characterization of the European philosophical tradition is that it consists of a series of footnotes to Plato". I think he might well have been right about this. Here is another thing that I also think is probably correct: we are all philosophers, whether we know it or not, and whether we have ever picked up a book of philosophy or not. Another twentieth-century philosopher, Ludwig Wittgenstein, said something very much like that, or at least something that implied it. What he didn't explicitly add, although it is clearly what he meant, was that most of us are very *bad* philosophers.

We are all philosophers in at least this sense. We are the products of culture, and the way we think is a reflection of this culture. Maybe we are not the exclusive products of culture; our biological heritage also has a massive role to play in shaping us. However, much of what we are – the way we think, what we desire, the values we endorse – we are because of the culture in which we have grown up. But cultures are, in part, expressions of one or another philosophy or system of ideas. As a result, each one of us, during the process of enculturation, has become the advocate or opponent of a collection of philosophical theses concerning ourselves and our place in the world. Often, we are also the unwitting victim of philosophical errors and confusions embodied in our culture. Often, indeed typically, we are blissfully unaware of these philosophical claims or confusions. The influence they exert on us is tacit rather than explicit; subterranean rather than overt. Nevertheless, we embody these philosophical claims, confusions and errors because our culture embodies them; and we are the products of this culture. Philosophy holds us all in its vice-like grip, whether we are aware of it or not.

This may strike you as implausible. I am going to try to convince you of it as the book proceeds. But the first thing I want to argue is that, in the style of Whitehead, probably "the safest general characterization" of the world today – and not just our culture – is as a series of footnotes not to Plato, but to a dispute that began with Plato's teacher Socrates and a man called Protagoras.

History, it is often said, is written by the winners. The history of philosophy is no exception; and you have only to read Plato's dialogues to know who the winner was in this particular case. Socrates never wrote any books. He left that to his star pupil, Plato. Plato wrote lots of them: mostly dialogues in which Socrates was the principal protagonist and almost invariably the winner, except for a disputed loss by split-decision at the hands of an ageing, but still very tasty, opponent called Parmenides in a book of the same name. This miscalculation apart, Socrates apparently picked his opponents very carefully. The thing that strikes any undergraduate student when they first pick up one of Plato's dialogues is just how inept Socrates' opponents are: just how puerile are their questions, just how inane are their responses to Socrates' questions. One can't help but be reminded of the later stages of Muhammad Ali's career, when he contented himself with fighting no-hopers (in a replication of Joe Louis's *bum of the month* programme). Most of Socrates' opponents appear as hapless as a Richard Dunn, hopelessly outclassed by Socrates' pot-bellied, snub-nosed, version of Ali.

So, it is reasonably safe to suppose that Plato's dialogues were written with the aim of making Socrates look better than he was. Moreover, most of what we know about Protagoras we know only through his appearance in Plato's dialogues – in particular, the *Protagoras* – where, as was Plato's custom, he was the featured bum of the month. So one should treat with caution the characterization of him contained therein. With suitable caution, then, Protagoras was a *sophist*. Sophists were professional educators of a sort. Their remit, however, was not to teach people how to find the truth, but how to win arguments – at least, this is Plato's spin on what they did. This ability they called "rhetoric". According to Plato, the sophists didn't have much time for the truth. Protagoras, at this time the undisputed heavyweight champion of the sophists, reportedly claimed that "Man is the measure of all things". Socrates' victory over Protagoras was therefore spun by Plato – in a way that might make even Alistair Campbell blush – as a victory over all the sophists and, by extension, a victory over the idea that man is the measure of all things.

What exactly did Protagoras mean by his (alleged) claim? Plato thinks there were two things he meant. The first was a claim about truth; the second a claim about value. The first claim would be that truth is relative to us. What is true or false depends on what we believe, on what we think is true. Is the earth round or flat? Well, it all depends on what we believe. If we believe it is round then it is round. But if we believe that it is flat, it is flat. This is Plato's construal of what Protagoras believed, of course, and I think we should treat this imputation with caution: for it is a truly asinine doctrine that today can find a home only in university English and cultural studies departments.

The other thing that Protagoras might have meant by his claim that "Man is the measure of all things" is a claim not about truth but about value. As such, Protagoras' claim is an expression of what later became known as *moral relativism*. This is a claim about the nature of right and wrong. It says that what is right and what is wrong is relative to "man" – Protagoras used the term *anthrōpos*, meaning human beings rather than specifically male human beings. "Man" in this context can mean either individual people or societies as a whole. The claim is based on the obvious idea that different people, and different cultures, can have different ideas about what's right and wrong. This was obvious even in Protagoras' time. The Greeks burned their dead; the Callatians ate them. The (ancient) Greeks practised infanticide, whereas we tend to take rather a dim view of that today. In the West, we are generally opposed to the mutilation of women's genitalia, but in parts of Africa that is positively *de rigeur*. Everyone knows that different cultures have different ideas about what is right and what is wrong. That claim is scarcely contestable. Protagoras' claim, however, amounts to much more than this. His claim is that what people think or believe about right and wrong exhausts everything there is to know about right and wrong. This is a strange and perplexing doctrine.

The doctrine, in effect, is that claims of right and wrong are elliptical. In this sense they are like claims concerning legality or illegality. It makes no sense to say that driving on the right-hand side of the road is illegal. Whether this is true depends on where you are. The claim is true in the United Kingdom but false in the United States. Claims about whether an act is legal and illegal involve implicit reference to a culture or society in which that act takes place. It makes no sense to say: OK, I understand that driving on the right-hand side of the road is illegal in the UK but legal in the US – but who is right about this? The idea of a culture-independent right or wrong makes no sense with legal statutes. Legal statutes are essentially culture relative.

Protagoras, in effect, argues that the same is true of moral rules or principles. There are no culture-independent standards of right and wrong. It makes no more sense to say "female genital mutilation is wrong" than it does to say "driving on the right-hand side of the road is illegal". It all depends, crucially, on where you are. You have no doubt heard the expression "When in Rome, do as the Romans do". The inspiration for this saying was Protagorean. For Protagoras, moral right and wrong reduce to the practices adopted in a culture. Right and wrong are, in this strong sense, culture-relative.

This makes moral values very different from facts. The Greeks of Protagoras' time thought the earth was flat, unless they were bright sparks like the Pythagoreans, who thought it was round (or the Presocratic philosopher, Anaximander, who thought it was a cylinder). But the shape of the earth is not simply a matter of what people happen to believe about it. The fact that everyone in a given culture believes that the earth is flat makes not the slightest difference to the actual shape of the earth. The shape of the earth is, in this sense, objective and independent of our beliefs about it. If Protagoras is right, then moral values are not like this at all. Moral right and wrong ultimately reduce to what people believe is right and wrong. Since what people believe to be right and wrong varies from culture to culture, so too does what actually is right and wrong.

Moral objectivism and the world of forms

If Protagoras was, in this sense, a moral relativist, Socrates, and by extension Plato, was a moral objectivist. Relativists believe that there is nothing more to right and wrong than what people believe about right and wrong, or to the practices erected on those beliefs. Moral objectivists deny this. For objectivists, right and wrong exist objectively and independently of what we happen to think about them and independently of how we happen to behave. Even if everyone thought that female genital mutilation ("female circumcision", as it is euphemistically known) is a good thing to do, it might still be morally wrong (and, for that matter, vice versa). Similarly, even if everyone thinks that the earth is flat, it might still be round (and, again, vice versa). For the objectivist, moral values are, to this extent, like scientific facts. Their existence is objective and independent of what people think or believe about them.

Socrates, as I have said, was the winner in this dispute. Plato went on to develop Socrates' objectivism by giving it a metaphysical basis in a world of what Plato called *forms*. In the sense employed by Plato, forms are, in effect, perfect exemplars of things. Consider, for example, a circle. Plato argued that in any physical circle there would always be some imperfection – no matter how slight – that made it fall short of being a perfect circle. No physical circle is ever truly circular: no matter how carefully it is drawn or constructed, it is only an approximation of a true circle. Nonetheless, we all recognize these approximations as being examples of circles. How do we do this if we have never, in fact, encountered a true circle? Plato argued that we must have implicit knowledge of something that is a perfect circle. Since all physical circles fall short of this standard of perfection, the perfect circle must be non-physical. He called it the form – the *eidos* – of the circle.

The same sort of reasoning Plato applied to all genuine kinds or categories of things. No horse is perfect: no matter how strong, fast or well-proportioned it is, it will always fall short of perfection to some degree or other. Nonetheless, we are perfectly capable of recognizing any given horse as a horse. Therefore, Plato thought, we must be implicitly comparing them to something that is a perfect horse: the non-physical form (or *eidos*) of the horse. This form of the horse is not part of the physical world but, rather, part of the non-physical world of forms. Circles, horses, dogs, trees, humans: according to Plato, the same logic applies. Since any physical example of these falls short of perfection, we must suppose there is a perfect exemplar of each kind inhabiting the non-physical world of forms. It is, roughly speaking, the resemblance each physical thing bears to its perfect exemplar that makes it belong to the kind – circle, horse, dog, tree or human – to which it, in fact, belongs.

Or, as Plato put it, each individual horse participates in the form of the horse; and each individual human being participates in the form of the human, and so on. The same is true of any genuine kind or category of thing. Of course, not all kinds or categories are genuine. The category of "things that have been in my kitchen" is not, we can assume, a real or genuine category: it is a purely artificial one made up by me a moment ago to illustrate the difference between real and artificial categories. However, Plato thought that for every genuine category or kind there is a form: and what makes something a member of the kind to which it belongs is its participation in this form. Indeed, by parity of reasoning, if we assume (which actually probably isn't true) that the category of "actors", "pop stars" and "society girls" are real categories, it would seem there would have to be non-physical perfect actors, non-physical perfect pop stars, and non-physical perfect society girls in this world of forms, sitting there for all eternity waiting for Lyndsay Lohan, Britney Spears and Paris Hilton to instantiate them to some or other imperfect degree.

The world of forms, according to Plato, is eternal and unchanging, and consists in the essences of things. In the actual physical world, the realm of the transient and ephemeral, objects instantiate these forms or essences only to a limited, imperfect, degree. Consequently, all physical things are flawed. But the forms or essences are not. Thus, Plato reasoned, the world of forms is both more real and more valuable than the real world. Trapped in the physical world, he argued, we are like prisoners chained in a cave, and our knowledge, or what we like to think of as our knowledge – for Plato it falls far short of that – of what is going on around us is like knowledge of the shadows cast by a fire on the walls of the cave. The goal of philosophy is to lead the prisoners out of the cave. Initially, we are blinded by the intensity of the light. But we learn to look first on objects illuminated by the light of the sun; and eventually we might even learn to look at the sun itself. The objects illuminated by the sun are the forms or essences of things. And the sun is one particular form: the most important of all forms – the form of the good. The world of forms, according to Plato, is a hierarchically structured world: a pyramid of forms. At the apex of the pyramid, the most real and valuable thing that does, or could ever, exist is the form of the good.

You might think that this theory is far-fetched. I'm inclined to agree. Nevertheless, its influence has been enormous. Most importantly, Plato was the first person ever to make intelligible, and then give intellectual respectability to, the idea of a non-physical realm of reality – indeed a realm that was more real and valuable than the physical world. This view was developed further by the neo-Platonist Plotinus. Plotinus identified the world of forms with, in effect, God, although he didn't explicitly call it God. The job was completed in the fourth century CE by Augustine, who used the conceptual framework created by Plato to introduce into early Christian thought the now familiar apparatus of souls, heaven and so on. These ideas may be familiar now, but they weren't in Augustine's day. Prior to Augustine, Christians believed in a purely physical afterlife, oriented around the idea of resurrection of the physical body. And indeed, in some Christian sects – Catholicism providing the most obvious example – this idea of a purely physical afterlife has proved particularly tenacious. The non-physical tenor of modern Christianity was introduced by Augustine, and this he derived from Plato. Modern Christianity is, to this extent, Platonic. This is just one more example of the extent to which many of us are unwitting philosophers.

Fundamentalism: the degenerate form of objectivism

There is a clear and unambiguous historical connection between Platonism and Christianity. However, for our purposes, what is important is a deeper connection: not between Platonism and Christianity but between Platonism and all religions. More accurately, the connection we need to explore is between Platonism and a certain way of thinking about religion in general.

As we have seen, Plato, and his mentor Socrates, were moral objectivists. That is, they believed that moral goodness exists objectively and independently of our beliefs, desires, opinions and practices. Moral goodness does not reduce to what we believe about it, or the practices we follow on the basis of these beliefs. What is good does not, in any way, depend on us. The same is true of moral badness or moral wrong. Although he did toy with the idea of negative forms in his most famous work, the *Republic*, Plato eventually decided he didn't want the form of evil populating his perfect world of forms. So he thought of moral wrong or evil not as a real presence in the world, but an absence of a real presence: the absence of the form of the good. However, for our purposes, this little wrinkle is insignificant. To the extent that moral goodness is an objective matter, and to the extent that its presence or absence is also an objective matter of fact, then moral badness, wrong or evil is also an objective matter. And this is what we need for our purposes: moral objectivism is the idea that moral right and wrong are objective matters of fact, independent of anyone's beliefs, opinions, attitudes or practices. This is something with which Plato would have agreed. Indeed, it is something on which he would have insisted.

This way of thinking about right and wrong is also characteristic of many religions: in the world of today Christianity and Islam provide the most obvious examples, but it is a guiding theme of most religions, certainly all theistic ones. Goodness is recorded, or on some versions constituted, by the word of God. It doesn't matter what we think of this word: whether we agree with it or disagree with it, hear it or refuse to hear it. If it is the word of God, then its truth does not in any way depend on our assent or acknowledgement. The word of God is eternally and necessarily true, and our attitude towards it – whether we be saints or sinners – is irrelevant to this truth. This way of thinking about religion is an expression of *fundamentalism*.

Therefore objectivism and fundamentalism seem to share at least this: they both believe in the existence of objective right and wrong. So, the question we must now look at is: what is the precise nature of the relation between objectivism and fundamentalism?

The answer is not difficult to discern: fundamentalism is objectivism without the argument. I know I have been less than complimentary about Socrates' and Plato's arguments. Personally, I don't think they are very good arguments, and if pushed I can give reasons for this belief of mine. However, whether I am right – and who knows, perhaps I'm not – doesn't matter for present purposes. Even if I am correct, there is something you can never take away from Socrates and Plato: *at least they tried.* That is what philosophy is all about: trying to develop arguments in favour of what you believe, and never simply being content with what you believe. Sometimes you are trying to convince someone else of your beliefs. Then the goal is to provide reasons better than your opponents and so win the argument. But there doesn't have to be anyone else involved. Sometimes you are trying to convince yourself of a particular view; and the goal is then to try to provide arguments for that view that in your honest, but of course fallible, opinion are better than the arguments against it. Philosophy is all about arguments, and without them it is nothing. Socrates and Plato were among the first to understand this. And that is why they are justifiably counted among the greats, even if you don't think their arguments actually work.

Philosophy is therefore anathema to fundamentalism. This is as true of Socratic–Platonic objectivism as it is of Protagorean relativism. Socrates and Protagoras disagreed deeply about the nature of reality and the nature of morality, but both of them provided arguments for what they believed. And to the extent that these arguments were good ones, they were capable of defending – rationally defending – what they believed. In no instance did they simply resort to "that's just the way it is" or "because I say so". Philosophy is in the business of providing arguments. But fundamentalism is in the business of not providing them: indeed, of stopping them in their tracks. A fundamentalist "justification" – if I may use the term loosely – is one step removed from "because I say so". Indeed, it's not clear that there is even a step here. Why do you believe P? It doesn't matter what P stands for. The philosopher replies by at least trying to provide an argument. If he does not, he or she is not, in this case at least, doing philosophy. The fundamentalist replies by saying: "God says so. God is in favour of P". If pushed on why he or she thinks God is in favour of P, the fundamentalist is likely to claim that this is what God says in this or that holy text, which is, of course, simply another version of "God says so". And if pushed on why we have reason to believe this holy text records the word of God, as opposed to other holy texts that also claim to record the word of God but are incompatible with this one, the fundamentalist is likely to respond: "Faith. Faith tells me that it is so". And this is just another way of saying: "I believe it. I say so". Once you do this, you may still be a philosopher in the sense that you are the subject of various philosophical ideas, conflations, confusions and errors. But you are now a bad philosopher. And you are a bad philosopher because you have given up on what philosophy is all about.

So, philosophy, whether objectivist or not, is anathema to fundamentalism. However, here's the rub. Because of certain human – let us call them – frailties, moral objectivism of the sort defended by Socrates and Plato has a natural tendency to degenerate into fundamentalism. The primary frailty in question is that many of us simply don't like arguments. More than that, we have little respect for them. Arguments just don't do it for us. Most of the time, we believe what we want to, and hang the arguments for or against those beliefs. If we have a choice between believing what we have good reason to believe, and believing what we want to believe or what we need to believe, we will come down on the side of desire and need (almost) every time. That is why philosophy is, as Wittgenstein once put, not so much a battle of the intellect but of the will. Philosophy is the battle to resist temptation. It is the fight to not believe something simply because you want or need to believe it.

The thing about arguments is that they are difficult. Thinking is hard. Sometimes it really hurts. It doesn't necessarily hurt in the sense that you don't like the conclusion you have reached by thinking, although that may be true also. Thought is no respecter of what we like. But thinking is also hard in the more basic way that even getting to a conclusion you like can hurt because it is such hard work. Humans don't like to hurt. Lazy and ungrateful creatures that we are, we simply don't like hard work.

One can hardly blame Socrates and Plato for this basic human predilection: they effectively invented philosophy precisely to subvert it. But, arguably, the tendency insinuates its way even into Plato's dialogues. Socrates won – and in particular he beat Protagoras – not because he had the better arguments but because his moral objectivism more closely aligned itself with some deeply felt human need. It may be that Protagoras was right – man is indeed the measure of all things – but that was not what we needed to hear. And to conflate what is true with what we need to be true is one of the truly human characteristics.

What were these needs? Who knows? Probably, the need to be right. Even more probably, the need to be better than other people. Almost certainly, the need to invent a worldview that afforded you at least some prospect of living on after death. It doesn't matter. Socrates won, Protagoras lost. And the world has never been the same since. Socrates and Plato gave us objectivism. But if the spectre of fundamentalism can insinuate its way even into Plato's dialogues, then this should tell us just how fragile objectivism is. So often our natural human slovenliness allows it to degenerate into fundamentalism. And, as a result, much of the human world, for much of human history, has been organized along explicitly funda-mentalist lines. No one needs reminding that this is as true of the world today as it has ever been.

Platonic objectivism is one of the defining ideas of what we now call the West. By Platonic objectivism, I'm not talking about the world of forms as such but the more general idea of the objectivity of value. The non-physical world of forms is just one way of trying to make sense of the idea that values are objective, and it's not a way I would particularly recommend. So, from now on, when I talk of "Platonic objectivism", "Plato's contribution" and so on, then you should understand me as talking about two things. First, there is the idea that values are objective. This is crucial, and not Plato's particular account of how they can be that way (the world of forms, etc.). Secondly, there is the idea that these values can be discovered through logical argument and unbiased evaluation of the evidence. Fundamentalism agrees with the first claim, but rejects the second out of hand. For fundamentalism, it is revelation rather than ration-ality that allows us to discover objective value.

The West is built, in part, on the idea that our most important values have objective validity, independent of what others, and even we, happen to think of them. But objectivism of this sort naturally degenerates into fundamentalism. The result is that fundamen-talism dogs our tracks: from its conceptual inception the West has been haunted by fundamentalism – the West is, in effect, always just a short intellectual step from fundamentalism.

Platonic objectivism, however, is not the only idea on which the West, as an intellectual or conceptual system, has been built. The second essential idea in the construction of the West was provided not by the ancient Athenians but by the Enlightenment French. This idea also has its own degenerate form. It is to this idea, and its degenerate form, that we now turn.

3. The Enlightenment project

Individualism and "the West"[1]

In this book, I am going to diagnose the condition of the modern West in terms of the opposition between two ideas that are basic to our intellectual and cultural heritage. However, each of these ideas has a degenerate form. Therefore, there are four axes along which the intellectual trajectory of the modern West can be charted. Ideologically speaking, the West – and each one of us citizens of the West – can be pulled in four different directions. The previous chapter introduced the first pair of axes, constituted by objectivism and its degenerate form, fundamentalism. This chapter introduces the other axes. The first of these is provided by the idea known as *individualism*. The second is made up of its degenerate form: *relativism*.

Part of the foundation of Western thought, and by extension Western social and political institutions, is provided by Plato's objectivism. Moral values – at least, our most important moral values – exist objectively, and independently of our beliefs, opinions, attitudes and practices. However, objectivism has a natural tendency to degenerate into something superficially similar but, in reality, very different – indeed, not only different but opposing: fundamentalism. Objectivism has a natural tendency to degenerate into fundamentalism because human beings have a natural tendency to be lazy and grasping. Fundamentalism comes about when we take the conclusions supplied by objectivism, and its method of rational enquiry underwritten by logical argument and unbiased gathering of evidence, and forget how we arrive at these conclusions. It is true, of course, that objectivists can, and often do, fall short of their own standards. This is to be expected if human beings are indeed lazy and grasping creatures. The important thing, however, is that, for objectivists, these standards of rational enquiry are there at least as ideals. Fundamentalists have no time for these standards. In essence, fundamentalism is objectivism that has no time for arguments.

However, objectivism is not the only essential constituent of the intellectual foundation of Western thought. One of the greatest experiments in the history of human civilization began in late-seventeenth-century France, was in full swing in the eighteenth century, and continues to this day. The experiment was referred to as the Enlightenment; and today, we refer to the result of this experiment as "the West". The West, in this sense, is not a place, but an idea, and that is what it should be taken to mean throughout this book. The West incorporates not only Western Europe and the United States, but also Australasia, South Africa and some other African states, South Korea, Japan, some parts of China and Indonesia, and large parts of Latin America. Its incorporation of these countries or areas is not, in general, complete. But its presence in all of them is significant enough to regard them as part of the West understood in the sense employed here.

If the West is not a place but an idea, what is this idea? The idea goes by a variety of names, but in this book I am going to refer to it as *individualism*. This term can, of course, mean different things to different people. I am going to use it to express only the following idea: a person's life typically goes best when it is lived from the inside – that is, when the person is allowed to choose how they are going to live it, and to live it on the basis of the choices they make. Accordingly, the most important thing in life is individual choice, and one of the most fundamental values that society must respect, and which it must be structured to reflect, is that of individual choice.

Of course, it is not always true that a person's life goes best when they are allowed to choose how to live it. That's why the claim was prefaced with the qualification, "typically". The choices we make are not always good ones and, as a result, we can often make an embarrassing mess of our lives. To see what the idea means, consider two societies. In the first one, people are allowed to choose how to live, in so far as this is possible. There will, of course, be restrictions on personal freedom: you can't simply choose any sort of life, especially if that life involves deliberately harming other people. So, the life of a mass-murderer, serial rapist, paedophile and so on is ruled out. But in this society, as long as you don't harm anyone else, you can pretty much choose how you are going to live. The second society is quite different. It is run in accordance with, and with the aim of safeguarding and preserving, certain values that it thinks everyone should adopt. These values are enforced in the sense that people are not allowed to lead a life that flouts them. The value of individual choice – if this society recognizes at all – comes a poor second to these other values.

The West is based on the thought that, in general, the lives of the people in the first society will be better than those in the second society: not always better, not necessarily better, but typically better. It might be thought that the West is, therefore, hostile to Plato's moral objectivism. Wouldn't Plato be more in favour of society number two – a society organized with a view to safeguarding commitment to a world of objective values? Many people have thought so, most notably Plato himself. However, this betrays a superficial understanding both of the West and, ultimately, of moral objectivism. If we look deeper, below the attractions of the surface, we will find out why the West and moral objectivism are more than just compatible; they are mutually reinforcing. Crucially, when properly understood, individualism incorporates Plato's idea of the objective validity of values. The key to understanding this lies in identifying what the word "better" means when we claim that the lives of those in the first society are better than those in the second.

Individualism and objectivism

Let us first look more closely at why we might be tempted to think that individualism and objectivism are mutually incompatible. According to individualism, the most important thing in any person's life is choice and, accordingly, one of the fundamental values that society must conserve is the value of individual choice. According to objectivism, on the other hand, there are values that exist prior to, and independently of, our choices, values that our choices must respect, and values that society must be structured to reflect. Individual choice is subservient to these values. Therefore it seems that we are inevitably led to the conclusion that individualism and objectivism are opposing values; and the visions of the individual and his or her relation to society embodied in each of these concepts are mutually incompatible. This conclusion, however, would be premature and superficial.

The key, as I said, is working out what the word "better" means in the claim that lives of the people in the first society will be better than those in the second. Much of the philosophical and political defence of the West has turned on two projects. First, there is the project of defending the intuition that the lives of the people in the first society would be better than those in the second. Secondly, there is the project of working out what counts as "better". The first project, in effect, is that of defending liberal democracy. The second project is that of providing an account of human welfare: what a good or valuable human life would look like. The second project is logically prior to the first. Unless you know – or at least have some idea – of what is the best sort of life for a human being to lead, you can't justify the claim that a society that allows human beings to live one sort of life is better than a society that does not.

One way of thinking about what makes a life "better" is hedonistic. That is, "better" is understood as "happier". It is still very common – particularly among social scientists – to suppose that human welfare consists exclusively in happiness. If so, a defence of liberal democracy would consist in trying to show that people in society one – the free society – would, in general, be happier than those in the authoritarian society number two.

However, this is not the only way to think about human welfare. And it is not the principal way that human welfare is understood in the Enlightenment project. Rather, the concept of individualism breaks down into two ideas, neither of which is essentially hedonistic. The first idea is that of *autonomy*: the ability to live your life as you see fit, in accordance with values you have freely chosen. This idea is, admittedly vague; but the second idea is even more so. *Self-realization* is the idea that you should, in so far as this is possible, maximize your abilities and potentialities: to become all you can be. Autonomy is valuable precisely because it promotes the possibility of self-realization. Autonomy is a necessary condition of self-realization in the sense that you cannot become all you can be if you are not given the opportunity to try. And to be given the opportunity to try to become all you can be, you must be allowed to choose to live your life in the way that you see fit. The life of being always told what to do is the life of a child. You cannot become all you can be until you learn to live as you see fit, and consequently to learn – and grow – from your mistakes.

Of course, it may be that self-realization is valuable only because people who have become all they can be are happier that those who are not. If this were true, then the value of self-realization would derive from its role in promoting happiness. However, it is doubtful that the Enlightenment ever involved the idea that happiness was, in this way, the ultimate value. On the contrary, on the most plausible way of thinking about the idea of Enlightenment and its justification, the Enlightenment is committed to resisting this idea.

If the Enlightenment project were based on the idea that happiness is our ultimate value, then it would, in effect, leave itself a hostage to fortune. To begin with, it might be very difficult to substantiate the claim that the people in society one – the free society – were any better off than those in authoritarian society number two. And even if they were, this is not necessarily true. There is no reason in principle why people living in an authoritarian society cannot be happier than those living in a free society, as long as the authoritarian society is sufficiently benign and the standard of living enjoyed by its citizens is of a sufficiently high standard. Therefore if the Enlightenment project were based on the idea that people in free societies were happier than those in authoritarian ones, the legitimacy of this project would depend on the open empirical question of whether it was possible to devise an authoritarian society whose members were happier than those living in free societies. But, typically, defenders of the Enlightenment do not think of it as hostage to empirical fortune in this way. The reason is that for them, at least implicitly, happiness was never the ultimate value of the Enlightenment.

That happiness was never the Enlightenment's ultimate value is sometimes lost in the recent idea that we should spread "freedom and democracy" throughout the world – by force if necessary. I agree that freedom and democracy are good things for people to have. And I support the idea that these should be spread throughout the world, although I suspect force of arms is not going to be a particularly efficient method of doing so. However, freedom and democracy are not good things because they necessarily make those who have them happier than those who do not. Free people in democratic regimes need not be any happier than un-free people in authoritarian regimes, just as adults are not necessarily happier than children (indeed, often it is quite the contrary).

We do a great disservice to the idea of the Enlightenment when we think it was all about happiness. It was about something quite different: it was about equipping people with the means of becoming all they can be. To do so, they had to be allowed to live the lives of adults and not children. And it is here that we find the reconciliation of Enlightenment individualism with Platonic objectivism.

It is crucial that we fix firmly in our minds the distinction between objectivism and fundamentalism. Fundamentalism is objectivism without the arguments. For Plato, fundamentalists are, in effect, like the prisoners in the cave, mistaking the shadows cast on the wall of the cave for objective truth and reality. This is the condition of people living in authoritarian societies. The reason is that living in such a way, where truth and values have to be accepted without question, leaves people living in authoritarian societies unequipped to ask questions. It leaves them unequipped to engage in rational enquiry underpinned by logical argument and unbiased evaluation of the evidence. If you are unable – unequipped – to do this, then you are not all you can be. The value of being all you can be – of fully realizing yourself in the Enlightenment sense – is precisely that it makes you the sort of person capable of discovering objective truth and value: it makes you the sort of person capable of acquainting yourself with Plato's world of forms.

This was the great insight of the Enlightenment; and ironically, it was an insight completely overlooked by Plato himself. Plato was famously attacked by the twentieth-century philosopher Karl Popper as en enemy of the "open" – that is, free – society. And Popper was quite correct. The ideal society envisaged by Plato was an authoritarian one where each person was allotted a place determined by his or her innate talents, and where all were subject to the philosopher kings – those with most insight into the world of forms. The genius of the Enlightenment was to take the Platonic project of rational enquiry into objective truth and value and see that this project was best pursued by people who were equipped to do so by living lives of autonomous self-realization. The principal merit of the free society bequeathed us by the Enlightenment is that it makes us the sorts of being that can pursue the Platonic project. That is why, at a less superficial level, the Enlightenment is the fulfilment of Plato rather than his rejection.

Relativism: the degenerate form of individualism

Therefore, the Enlightenment project is perfectly compatible with Platonic objectivism. Indeed, it arguably provides the best framework within which the Platonic project may be pursued. However, the connection between the two runs even deeper than this. Ultimately, the very idea of individualism does not make sense without Platonic objectivism; if our most important values do not have objective validity, then the idea of individualism, ultimately, makes no sense.

I have argued that objectivism naturally degenerates, owing to certain human failings, into fundamentalism: essentially, objectivism bereft of rational argument or empirical enquiry. Individualism also has its degenerate form: *relativism*. If objectivism, at least in the hands of human beings, is an unstable position, then so too is individualism. Crucially, however, individualism typically degenerates into relativism when we lose sight of the close connection between individualism and objectivism.

There is a certain fragility – more accurately, an instability – that lies at the heart of the Enlightenment project. The instability turns on the relation between autonomy and self-realization. The basic idea of self-realization is that you should maximize your abilities and potentialities, thus becoming all you can be. You do this – and herein we find the value of autonomy – through the choices you make and your willingness to learn from those choices. However, it can't be that any choice counts as self-realization. If anything you do counts as self-realization, then the idea of self-realization is vacuous. This point has been developed quite forcefully by Canadian philosopher Charles Taylor (1984, 1992).

Here are some of the choices you might make in your life with regards to just one aspect of it: your occupation. You might choose to become a surgeon, a lap dancer, a voluntary worker overseas, a lawyer, a hairdresser, a hit man, an estate agent, a prostitute, a dog walker, a university lecturer, a cage fighter, an epidemiologist, a gang member, a priest, a porn star, a florist, a pop singer, a malingerer and so on. All of these are choices you might make, and in making these choices your life takes on a certain shape and you realize yourself as being one sort of person rather than another. I'm not going to take a stand on which of these choices are the best ones, and which are the worst. However, surely, some of these choices must be better than others. If any type of self-realization is just as good as any other, then the idea of self-realization means nothing. If any type of self-realization is as good as any other, then it would be impossible to not realize yourself: it would be impossible to fail to become the best you can be. If anything counts as optimal self-realization, then whatever you do involves maximizing your abilities and potentialities. And so the idea of self-realization becomes vacuous. But autonomy is valuable to the extent that it promotes the possibility of self-realization: if self-realization is vacuous, then autonomy is worthless. But individualism is made up of the combination of the ideas of autonomy and self-realization, which means that individualism is the combination of a worthless and vacuous idea respectively. But the West is built on the idea of individualism. Therefore, the West would be built on a combination of the worthless and the vacuous. It seems the Enlightenment project is in conceptual tatters.

How do we avoid this? We avoid it by accepting that individualism only makes sense against a background of objectivism. What we need to do is ensure that not every form of self-realization counts as equally good as any other. And to ensure this, we need an objective system for ranking our choices: the choices we make in realizing ourselves. Not every choice we make is as good as any other. Some choices are better than others. Some choices are good ones, some are excellent ones; some are positively banal, and some are just plain stupid. The idea of self-realization requires a way of ranking choices, of evaluating them in such a way that some choices we make can be good ones and others bad. For, it is an unfortunate, inconvenient, but nonetheless necessary truth that if there is no such thing as a bad choice, then there is no such thing as a good choice either. Or, as American author Gore Vidal once put it: "It is not enough to succeed. Others must fail."

To sort the choices we make into the good, the bad and the ugly, we need a way of ranking those choices. And this leads us straight back to the Platonic idea of a system of values that is objective and independent of us. Far from being a rejection of Plato, the Enlightenment project seems to require Plato. And it seems to require Plato because it wouldn't make any sense without him. When properly understood, individualism both requires and incorporates the Platonic idea of the objectivity of (our most important) values. If the West is built on individualism it is therefore, at the same time, built on objectivism.

The problem is that we seem more and more determined to lose sight of this fact. Today, it is increasingly common to find individualism confused with its degenerate form. Just as objectivism has a degenerate form – a dogmatic fundamentalism – so too does individualism. The degenerate form of individualism is relativism. Relativism, very roughly, is the idea that all moral systems are equally valid. However, this general idea can also be applied to individuals and the lives they lead. Thus applied, relativism is the idea that all forms of life are equally viable and therefore equally valuable.

By "form of life" I mean not so much the particular, concrete, life that you choose to live, but the values embodied in the choices that allow you to live it. These values can manifest themselves in both gross and subtle ways, in connection with both the major life decisions that you make, and the small modifications you make to those decisions as your life unfolds. You choose to become a slacker who smokes dope all day rather than seek gainful employment. In this choice is embodied, generally in tacit, and presumably rather hazy, form a particular understanding of the value of life. You understand the bankruptcy of the values of the driven: the values that would see you up at the crack of dawn each day, constantly looking for the next mark, the new angle, the best way of advancing your career. Occasionally, you might see these people scurrying to work in the morning rush hour, and ask yourself "Why?" Why do they fill their lives with little goals: the meeting with Mr X at lunchtime to discuss the North American market; the presentation to investors at 3.00 p.m.; the dalliance with Miss Y after work? Perhaps they enjoy these things, perhaps they don't. They do them anyway. And eventually they will have children who will grow up and do pretty much the same things. Far better, you might think, to leave the rat race to the rats, and actually have some fun. Embodied in this choice is a certain conception of what is of value. The life that consists in the achievement of little goals is worthless. The life of fun – of hedonism – is far more valuable. The ultimate value in life, you have decided, explicitly or implicitly, is pleasure. And this, therefore, is the value you have decided to build your life around.

However, after some years, you might have cause to rue your choice, either bored with a life of unremitting hedonism, or lacking the financial means to successfully pursue it. Accordingly, you complete your education, seek gainful employment and start doing the things you swore you would never do. In this, we find a revision of the values that shape your life. Now you are building your life around new values. Maybe these new values concern your family, for you have come to acquire one. Now, you decide what is most important in life is not pleasure – although you hope your new life might still contain at least some of that – but providing for the security and future of your family.

Through our choices, our life comes to take on a certain form. And any form of life embodies values, for these are simply an implicit understanding of what is important, indeed what is most important, in life. In his or her choice of occupation, the chief executive of a multinational company that makes its money from despoliation of the environment embodies the understanding that what is important in life is to advance your own claims and those of your family over those of other people and other things. What come first are me and mine. This understanding is not restricted to choice of occupation. The mother who drives her only child to school – although it's merely half a mile down the road – in a huge 4×4 embodies this value, albeit in a slightly different way.

I am simply pointing out these values, and showing how they are exhibited in the choices we make. I am not criticizing them. However, I do think it is possible to criticize values. And this is precisely what the relativist denies. According to relativism, as it is applied to individuals, all forms of life are equally legitimate. If I choose to develop myself in one way rather than another, to live my life in accordance with one set of values rather than another, then this choice, and the values it embodies, is just as good as any other. With regard to forms of life, the relativist says not only "Let a thousand flowers bloom"; he also adds, "And every flower is just as good as any other".

This vapid form of relativism is not only seriously confused; it is, from the perspective of the Enlightenment, unintelligible. The core ideas of the Enlightenment – autonomy and self-realization, with the former acting as a precondition of the latter – only make sense if we have some objective system of value that we can use for ranking choices: a system that will allow us to recognize that some choices are better than others. Without this, the idea of self-realization makes no sense, and the value of autonomy is, therefore, undermined.

This means that the West is, in many ways, a confusing place to be. It is confusing in the sense that its products – us – are continually misunderstanding it. We persist in confusing the core Enlightenment idea of individualism with its degenerate form – a vacuous form of relativism – where this degenerate form is not simply an inaccurate expression of what the Enlightenment is all about; it is actually incompatible with what the Enlightenment is all about. Consequently, we persist in thinking of the freedom afforded us by the Enlightenment project as a freedom that consists in throwing off two thousand years of authoritarian objectivist hegemony. In fact, the Enlightenment requires the sort of moral objectivism first defined and defended by Plato. This however, we also continually confuse with its degenerate form: a dogmatic, and often rabid, fundamentalism.

So, the two central ideas that effectively define the West – individualism and objectivism – we persist in confusing with their degenerate forms – relativism and fundamentalism. Or, worse, we try to make these into their degenerate forms. But relativism and fundamentalism are, of course, incompatible: there is no way of reconciling these two views. Imagine telling a fundamentalist Islamic Imam, or a fundamentalist Christian preacher, to let a thousand flowers bloom because every flower is as good as any other; see how far you get. The post-Enlightenment West is a fractured and confusing place to be. And consequently, we – its products – are fractured and confused creatures.

4. Lightness and weight

The story so far

The most obvious question that emerges from the preceding discussion is, of course: what does any of this remotely have to do with fame? I am, in fact, getting to that. The purpose of this rather circuitous discussion of the nature of the West is to give us some sense of the predicament in which we products of the West find ourselves. In particular, what I have tried to show is that the West is the product of certain tensions. First of all, there is the tension between objectivism and individualism. These two ideas are, I have argued, compatible. Indeed, more than that, they actually support each other. However, unless we are very precise in our understanding of them, we can easily become confused and believe them to be incompatible. It is in this possibility that the tension between individualism and objectivism can be found: it is a tension that issues from a misunderstanding of these ideas. Secondly, both individualism and objectivism have a tendency to collapse into their degenerate forms: relativism and fundamentalism, respectively. It is to these tensions – between individualism and objectivism, and between each of these and their respective degenerate forms – and to a specific form of degeneration that the West can consequently undergo, that we have to look to properly understand the rise and rise of vfame.

In more detail, the argument so far has gone something like this. First, the West is the result of a philosophical experiment – one that we refer to as the Enlightenment – that began in late-seventeenth-century France. This experiment consisted in the attempt to combine the moral objectivism inherited from Plato with a kind of individualism that claimed that each person's life typically goes best when it is lived from the inside: that is, when the person is allowed to choose how to live it. The reconciliation of objectivism and individualism is based on the idea that allowing a person to live a life they have chosen, rather than one foisted on them from the outside, helps sharpen their rational and moral faculties, and so makes them the sort of person more capable of discovering and, crucially, defending the sorts of facts and values Plato thought of as present in the structure of reality. Moreover, more than being simply compatible, individualism requires objectivism in that without it its core rationale – the idea of self-realization – would make little sense. Nevertheless, despite being mutually compatible principles, individualism and objectivism coexist only in a constant state of tension owing to the permanent possibility of their being improperly understood: a typical occurrence.

This state of tension is exhibited in the tendency of both individualism and objectivism to degenerate into inferior forms. Largely owing to human laziness, and our aversion to things unpleasant, objectivism has a natural tendency to degenerate into fundamentalism: objectivism without the logical arguments and/or empirical evidence. Objectivism has a natural tendency to degenerate into fundamentalism because thinking – rational thinking subject to logical norms and empirical refutation – is hard. Often, it hurts. And we have a natural, and entirely understandable, tendency to shun what is hard or what hurts. How much easier we find it to recline in the gentle embrace of dogma.

Individualism also has a natural tendency to degenerate: into not fundamentalism but relativism. This degeneration occurs when we focus on the individualist ideal of living life as we choose it, according to values and principles we have freely undertaken, and lose sight of the purpose of this undertaking. The purpose is to make us better people: objectively better people. That is, the purpose is to make us the sort of people capable of discovering objective moral value and empirical truth. If we focus on the individualist arm of this project, and lose track of its objectivist underpinning, then our individualism will tend to degenerate into relativism. In essence, we have focused unduly on the process, and lost sight of the product of that process.

If this analysis is correct, then the West emerges as fundamentally unstable. Individualism and objectivism coexist in a constant state of tension, both with each other and with their respective degenerate forms. What we think of as the West is, and has been since its inception, a delicate juggling act: an attempt, and at its best a magnificent attempt, to keep both objectivist and individualist balls in the air, without allowing the degeneration of either into their inferior forms. Nietzsche once wrote in *Thus Spoke Zarathustra*, "one must still have chaos in oneself to give birth to a dancing star". And I think that to a considerable extent the greatness of the West – its strength and fecundity – is a result of the conceptual tension that lies at its core. The constant demand to balance individualism and objectivism consists in the requirement to give individualism as much of its head as circumstances allow, and the concomitant requirement to be continually vigilant with respect to those circumstances, to make sure they actually permit what you believe them to permit, and so on: this sort of tension and this sort of vigilance provide a rich soil from which the many and dazzling achievements of the West have sprung.

The idea I want to explore in this chapter is that the unstable, and often conflicted, nature of the Enlightenment project results in the unstable, and often conflicted, nature of its products: us. Precisely because we are products of the Enlightenment, each one of us is an amalgam, an often confused melange, of two different ways of thinking about ourselves. There is a part of us that is an individualist, and a part that is an objectivist, and the relative amount of each varies from person to person. And each of these parts of our character has a tendency to degenerate into relativist and fundamentalist forms respectively. As a result, we are, typically, unstable, and sometimes fractured creatures. Our lot, it seems, is never to be quite able to reconcile ourselves with ourselves.

Lightness and weight

In his novel *The Unbearable Lightness of Being*, the Czech novelist Milan Kundera, one of the more impressive products of the Enlightenment, supplies us with a metaphorical binary opposition that is very useful for framing our predicament: the opposition between *lightness* and *weight*. Kundera writes:

> The heaviest burden crushes us, we bend beneath it, it presses us to the ground. But in the love poetry of all centuries, the woman desires to receive the burden of the male body. The heaviest burden is, therefore, at the same time the image of the most intense fulfilment. The heavier the burden, the closer our lives come to the earth, the more they are real and true.
>
> On the other hand, the absence of weight makes the human being become lighter than air, he flies away, removed from the earth and his earthly being, and becomes only half real, his movements as free as they are insignificant.
>
> What then shall we choose? Lightness or weight?

Kundera traces this opposition back to Parmenides, an ancient Greek philosopher of the fifth century BCE. However, for our purposes, it provides a useful way of thinking about the opposition between individualism and objectivism. Here, we are trying to understand the opposition not as it figures in an abstract structural account of the Enlightenment West; rather, the goal is to understand how this opposition has become reflected in each one of us. That is, in this chapter, our focus switches from the nature of Enlightenment society to the nature of the Enlightenment individual. The idea is that as products of the West we come to reflect in our characters and our outlooks these features on which the West has been built. If the West is built on an opposition of individualism and objectivism, then that opposition will have become reflected in, or will have otherwise written itself upon, us. If individualism naturally tends to degenerate into relativism, and objectivism naturally tends to degenerate into fundamentalism, then these twin tendencies will similarly be reflected in us. Roughly, and in a sense to be made clear, I shall argue that Kundera's concept of lightness corresponds to the individualist strand of our character and outlook; Kundera's weight corresponds to their objectivist strand.

In this section, I am going to advance and defend a certain interpretation of the ideas of lightness and weight. The distinction, I am going to argue, can be captured in terms of the concept of *constitutive attachment* to the world outside you: in particular, to the values outside of you. Weight consists in being constitutively attached to one's values. Lightness consists in the absence of such attachments.

A life that is light is a life lived without any constitutive attachment to one's values. The notion of constitutive attachment pertains, first and foremost, to a certain way of understanding yourself: a certain form of self-understanding, as it is sometimes known. So, to live a life that is light is to understand yourself in a certain way: as standing in a certain type of relation to your values. Roughly, and in a sense to be made clear, it is to think of yourself as existing prior to and independently of, your values.

I argued earlier that the various life and lifestyle choices we make embody, sometimes explicitly but more often implicitly, the values we endorse. Your choices concerning the sort of job you get – or whether you get one at all – embody values. Your choices about where you live, who you marry (if you marry at all), the schools to which you send your children (if you choose to have them), the mode of transportation you employ, the books you read, the clothes you wear, the places you visit: in all of these choices we find the endorsement of certain values. Not all of these values are deep ones; some are trivial. And not all choices embody values to the same degree; the connection can range from entailment to slight association. Nevertheless, if you excavate any significant life choice far enough, you will eventually find a value or values that it embodies or presupposes. In such choices also, we shall find concomitant rejection of other values, for to endorse a given value is to reject those other values that are incompatible with it.

Think about the values you have endorsed through the choices you have made in your life. Now ask yourself: what is the relation between me and those values? On the one hand there is, it seems, you. On the other are the choices you make and, consequently, the values you endorse. But what is the relation between the two? What is the relation between the person who, through the choices they make, endorses and rejects values and the values that he or she endorses or rejects?

For example, suppose that when you left school you decided to go to university. There you chose a degree course that you didn't really enjoy – in fact you hated it – because you assumed, rightly or wrongly, that there would be a good job waiting for you at the end of it. Embodied in this choice is a certain way of thinking about life and what is important in it. Embodied in this choice, that is, are certain values that pertain to how you rank the relative importance of present and future. There are, presumably, other values also embodied in your choice, but let us just focus on this one. The value embodied in your choice tells you, in effect, that a future of long-term security is more important than a present of unalloyed enjoyment. You really wanted to do the degree in filmmaking, but were you to do so your future prospects would be, to say the least, uncertain. So you stuck with the marketing course that you hated. In making a choice like this, you reveal that, in your system of values, the future is ranked more highly then the present. You orient your life around the future rather than the present because, for you, the future is more valuable. This is perhaps not the most basic value that you might have, but it is an important one: far deeper and more consequential than many suppose.

Sometimes, you cast wistful glances at your friends: those devil-may-care, look-after-today-and-tomorrow-will-look-after-itself types on the filmmaking degree. But could you really be one of them? This is a question about the relation between you – the person you are – and your values. The question is not: would you still be the same person if you hadn't gone to university? That is a question about the relation between you and a certain worldly institution: the university. And, for what it's worth, the answer to this question is, I think, clearly yes. Our question concerns the relation between you and your values rather than things in the world in general. Thus, the question is: if you valued the present more highly than you valued the future, then would it still be you? Could you value the present more highly than the future – could you be one of those devil-may-care types – without changing who you essentially are and becoming, in effect, a different person?

This question is intended as a question about how you under-stand yourself – the sort of thing you take yourself to be – rather than a question about what you actually are. Philosophers have, for quite some time, been interested in what they call the question of *personal identity*. This is the question of what makes you the person you are (and concomitantly, what distinguishes you from everyone else). No one has really ever identified an account of personal iden-tity, in this sense, that is demonstrably correct, and some now even question whether there is a correct account. However, this does not matter for our purposes because this is not our question. Our question is a subtly different one. Our question does not concern who or what you really are; it concerns only how you *think* of yourself – what sort of thing you take yourself to be. That is what is crucial for our purposes. In particular, do you or do you not understand yourself as, in principle, existing prior to and independently of the values that you endorse? Thus, suppose you, in fact, value the future more highly than the present. Our question is not: could you value the present more highly than the future and still be the same person? In my opinion, the answer to this question is a qualified yes: if you are ever the same person – if there is such a thing as the same person – then you could swap around your relative ordering of future and present without changing who you are. But this is not our question. Our question is: do you think you could come to value the present more highly than the future? Could you do this without becoming, in effect, a different person? This question pertains to how you think about yourself, not to what you really are, assuming you really are anything.

The distinction between lightness and weight consists in a distinction between two different ways of thinking about yourself rather than a distinction between two different sorts of things that you might, in principle, turn out to be. Your life is light if you think of yourself in such a way that you could, in principle survive a transformation of your major – your most deeply held – values. Your life is light if, according to your self-conception, you could survive such a transformation without becoming a different person: without becoming, in effect, someone else. To think of yourself in this way is to endorse a certain conception of the relation between you and your values: even your most deeply held values. According to this conception, you exist prior to and independently of your values. The values you endorse in your life and your choices – even the most deeply held of your values – are reflections or expressions of a person who exists prior to and independently of them. That person is you. The values you endorse are reflections of the person you are, but they do not make you the person you are. The dependency is one-way, and runs from the person to their values: you choose the values you choose because of who you are; you are not, conversely, who you are because of the values you choose. According to this way of thinking about yourself, your values do not run deeply to enter into your identity as the person you are. Rather, they merely reflect a person who already exists prior to and independently of the values that he or she endorses. And they, therefore, reflect a person who would still exist even if those values were rejected and new ones endorsed in their place.

So, more generally, the life of a person is a light one if the following principle is true of it: according to the way the person understands themselves, it is possible to vary the values that the person endorses – even the most serious or most deeply held of his values – without altering the identity of the person in question. What this means, in effect, is that the person understands herself as not constitutively attached to her values: the person has no constitutive attachments to her values because they do not make her the person she is but are merely reflections of the person she already is, prior to and independently of those values. We might think of the values that this person endorses as like a coat she can put on or take off. Whether she is wearing the coat or not, she is essentially unaltered by it: it is still the same person that is present whether or not she is wearing the coat. It is true that the coat might be put on or taken off only in the most exceptional of circumstances; the coat might be a constant sartorial accompaniment. But it is still true that whether or not the coat is ever taken off, it can still be taken off in principle without altering the identity of the person who wears it.

If you think this principle is true of you – if you think of your values as a function of your choices, and your choices as things that you endorse or reject without altering who you really are – then your life is a light one. One of the more famous representatives of this position is the existentialist philosopher Jean-Paul Sartre. Sartre (1958) argued that your endorsing any particular value is always a matter of your choice: an expression of the freedom that, Sartre thought, defines you. You can endorse a value on one day, and this is a function of your freedom to choose. But to continue to endorse this value on subsequent occasions – the next day, and the day after – is also, and to no lesser extent, a matter of choice. The real you is the one that chooses, and not any of the choices you make. What you are is defined by what you are not; you are not any of the things of which you are conscious, including your choices and the values they embody. And this means that the real you is, ultimately, nothing at all: "a wind blowing from nowhere toward the world", as Sartre (1947: 31) once put it. This is an accurate and powerful expression of the logical culmination of a life that is light.

Your life is heavy, on the other hand, if you understand your-self as constitutively attached to your values. Again, I emphasize that this is not a claim about what you actually are; in the absence of a demonstrably correct account of personal identity no one is really sure what you actually are. Rather, it is a claim about what you understand yourself to be. Your life is heavy when you under-stand yourself in such a way that without the values you endorse you would no longer exist as the same person. Let's go back to our choice of which to value more, the past or the future. You value the future, and so are aspiring to a job in marketing instead of film-making. You ask yourself: could I have been any different? Could I have been like my friends who value the present most, and think that the future will take care of itself? If, after much thought, you decide that you couldn't – that without your obsessive focusing on the future you would not be you – then you think of yourself as constitutively attached to this valuing of the future; this value you ascribe to the future is part of what makes you who you are, or, at least, so you think. Thus, according to this way of thinking about yourself, your values – or at least some of the more serious ones – enter into the identity of the person you are: they constitute who you now are.

This may be an implausible example. Many of us change our relative assessments of the value of present and future. It is characteristic for these assessments to change, for obvious reasons, at least twice in the course of a lifetime. But we don't have to look far for more plausible examples. The religious fundamentalist who proclaims that he could not exist without his belief in God and without his endorsement of the values God has ordained, is providing an all too familiar expression of the idea that life – his life at least – is heavy. Far from merely reflecting the predilections of a self or person who already exists prior to and independently of them, the religious fundamentalist understands himself as being constituted by the values he endorses. He is, in effect, saying that in the absence of commitment to the values of his religion, there may be a person inhabiting his body, but that person would not be him. Your life is heavy when there are certain values that are so important to you that you believe that you – the person you are – could not exist without them. Again, this is a claim about how you think of or understand yourself rather than a claim about what you actually are. Whether a person is or can be actually constituted by their values is not an issue we need to address. What is crucial is whether a person can think of themselves in this way. If they do, then their life is a heavy one, at least according to the way of understanding Kundera's distinction that I have developed here.

So, whether your life is a light or heavy one depends on how you understand yourself, and, in particular, how you understand the relation you bear to your values. Your life is light if, according to the way you understand yourself, you have no constitutive attachments to your values because they do not make you who you are. Your life is heavy if, according to the way you understand yourself, you do have constitutive attachments to at least some of your values – because these values do make you who you are.

Choice, identification and the Enlightenment

After introducing the distinction, Kundera poses a question: which should we choose – lightness or weight? Kundera's novels have done more than anything to convince us of the folly of thinking that this question admits of a straightforward answer. Both sorts of lives have their advantages and disadvantages. A life that is light is, in itself, no better and no worse than a life that is heavy; the lives are just different. In this section, I am concerned not with evaluating the relative merits of each sort of life (that will be the subject of Chapter 5) – but with tracing the connection between these lives and the analysis of the Enlightenment developed in the preceding chapters.

To begin with, there is a deep, and I think interesting, connection between the light conception of the person – according to which a person has no identity-constituting attachments to their values – and the individualist strand of Enlightenment. Simply put, a life that is light is the – or at least *one* – logical culmination of an individualism unconstrained by any objectivist counterbalance. As we have seen, according to individualism your life goes best, typically, if not always or necessarily, when it is lived from the inside: when it is you that chooses how to live it. Your life goes best when you have authority over your life in the sense that you are the *author* of it. But an author – one and the same author – can write many books. For you to be an author, it is not what you write that is important, but that you write. Of course, to be a good writer is a different matter, but this directs us back towards objective standards of evaluation characteristic of the objectivist strand of the Enlightenment. And this is a point to which we shall turn shortly. But, at the moment, we are trying to understand what a life that is individualistic, and unconstrained by objectivist counterbalance, would look like. The answer to this question is, I think, it would look like a life that is light.

If we focus purely on the individualist strand of Enlightenment, then what is important is *that* you choose and not *what* you choose. Individual choice or autonomy, and self-realization through that autonomy, is of overriding importance. However, as we have seen, implicated in your choices are values, whether deep or trivial. Therefore, if it is your choosing rather than the specific content of your choices that is important from the perspective of the individualist strand of Enlightenment – and, again, I emphasize that this is individualism unconstrained by objectivist counterbalance – then, from that perspective, what specific values you endorse are not as important as the fact that you endorse values. Thus, implicated in the individualist strand of Enlightenment is this idea: what you are, in your essence, is a maker of choices and, consequently, an endorser of values. But your identity as the specific person you are is not determined by the specific content of the choices you make and the values that you thereby endorse. From the individualist perspective, which life you choose is not important in the sense that it does not define you. What is important – what does define you – is that you choose. You choose one life, but you could have chosen another. It would still be you living that other life. In this sense, you exist prior to, and independently of, your choices. You are that which chooses, and therefore that which values, but the content of your choices and the specific values embodied in them, do not constitute who you essentially are. In this fairly straightforward way, the logical culmination of the individualist strand of Enlightenment is the light conception of the person.

The connection between the objectivist strand of the Enlightenment and the heavy conception of the person is less straightforward but, I think, ultimately no less compelling. According to the objectivist strand, there are values that exist prior to, and independently of, my choices. These values, rather than simply being embodied in my choices as the individualist claims, also provide standards by which my choices might be evaluated. If my choices fail to reflect or otherwise live up to these values, then my choices are, in some respect or other, defective. Moreover, they also provide standards in terms of which I – and not just my actions – may be evaluated. If I fail to recognize, and be motivated by, what is good, I have, in this case, failed as a moral agent. If I fail to recognize, and be motivated by, the beautiful, then, in this case at least, I have failed as an aesthetic being. These objective values exist prior to me and provide a standard by which I may be judged. The measure of me as a person is determined by the extent to which I live up to – reflect in my thoughts and deeds – these values that exist objectively and independently of me. What is most important in life is not, *contra* individualism, simply to choose; rather, it is to make good choices, where this is understood as a matter of conforming to or otherwise reflecting objective values.

What, however, is involved in my actions' reflecting these objective and independent values? The most obvious route between this sort of objectivism and the heavy conception of the person lies in the fact that the latter can be used as a way of interpreting the former. The relation between the two is not one of entailment; rather, it is that the heavy conception of the person provides a natural way – although not the only way – of understanding why objectivism might be true.

According to objectivism, one's choices should – are supposed to – conform to values that exist independently of them. Someone whose life is light can, of course, also do this. They can make their choices conform to values that they take to exist independently of them; it is just that these values – according to the way they understand themselves – do not enter into the identity of who they are. According to their self-understanding, they exist prior to their choices, and so exist independently of the values embodied in those choices. However, this light conception of the relation between a person and his values does leave us with a puzzle. The puzzle concerns the *authority* of those values: the authority of those values over the person who endorses them.

Let us suppose I understand my self as light, but I also think there are objective values. That is, I acknowledge the existence of objective values but don't think my adherence to those values makes me who I am. I am, as a matter of fact, a good person. But I could have been a bad one. Nonetheless, because I acknowledge the existence of objective values, I accept that these are values that I should accept or endorse. The puzzle concerns the status of this "should". Why "should" I endorse these values? If I can endorse these values only through my choices, and I am free to choose, then precisely why should I endorse these values? Understanding the authority of moral values – understanding the sense in which they can be binding on us – is one of the hardest tasks in philosophy. And it is not clear that any answer hitherto provided is adequate. The existentialists – those champions of individualism unconstrained by objectivism – argued that there is no robust sense in which moral values can have authority over us. In this Godless age – and for the existentialists that is precisely what it is – to suppose that moral values have authority over us is to believe in a God-made law but not in the God who made it.

However, while there may be no entirely satisfactory answer to the question of the authority of moral values, the heavy conception of the person does at least provide us with *an* answer. Let us suppose I understand myself as heavy. If so, then I will think of the values that I endorse – at least the deep or serious ones – as entering into the identity of who I am. My values are part of me – or, at least, this is how I understand myself. But if this is true, then in failing to live up to these values I am, in an important sense, failing to be who I am. A failure to endorse my values is a failure to live up to who I am. A moral failure is also an existential failure: a failure to be, if you like, true to myself. Ultimately, if our form of self-understanding is a heavy one, my values have authority over my choices because my values make me who I am; and *I* have authority over myself.

Therefore, the connection between the objectivist strand of Enlightenment and the heavy conception of the person is more logically complex than the corresponding connection between the individualist strand and the light conception of the person. However, ultimately, I think the connection is just as clear and compelling. Trying to combine the light conception of the person with the idea of objective values leads to a difficult, and perhaps intractable, problem of explaining the authority that these values could have over such a person. The heavy conception of the person at least provides an answer to this problem, although whether that answer is ultimately acceptable is not something we can discuss here. Therefore, while the objectivist strand of Enlightenment and the heavy conception of the person are not mutually entailing, they are mutually reinforcing.

The fractured self

The above account of the distinction between lightness and weight is intended as a descriptive analysis rather than an evaluation. I am not claiming that the life of lightness is better than that of weight, or that the life of weight is better than that of lightness. On the contrary, as we shall see, the life of each taken in isolation from the other is a rather sad one. The genius of the West lay in this realization. That is what the Enlightenment, in effect, was all about. The Enlightenment consisted in the realization that societies are best formed from an appropriate combination of objectivism and individualism: a delicate juggling act of individual choice and objective value. But this realization is also reflected at the level of the individual. The individual's life goes best when it is an appropriate combination of lightness and weight. Working out what "appropriate" means is, of course, the hard part. Different people will disagree strongly over this, and they may have legitimate (if not compelling) reasons for their disagreement. And even the same person at different times in her life can have different understandings of what a healthy balance between lightness and weight amounts to; and, indeed, both different times and different people may call for a different balance. The idea of balance here is not a mathematical calculation of forces; it is more like a juggling act. And like any juggling act, it is perhaps not the sort of thing that can be sustained indefinitely.

The act reasserts itself over and over again in post-Enlightenment thought. Indeed, much philosophy and political theory of the past three hundred years can be seen as a reiteration of this basic distinction and its consequences: a pendulum that swings back and forth between individualism and objectivism at the level of society and lightness and weight at the level of the individual. The dispute between liberals and Marxists is merely one version of this act. At various times, forms of individualism are asserted only to find themselves quickly opposed by forms of objectivism, and the act plays on. In essence, the debate is always this: what is the ideal ratio of objectivism to individualism? How much objectivism do we need, and how much individualism can be permitted?

The same is true, as we should expect, when the debate occurs at the level of the individual rather than society. For example, perhaps the primary dispute in contemporary political philosophy has been between liberals and communitarians. This dispute is typically fought at the level of the individual. The communitarians accuse the liberals of presupposing an "unencumbered" conception of the self: a vision of the self or person as existing without any constitutive attachments to values or other persons. In place of this, communitarians advocate a view of the self that sees it as constituted by its relations to its values and the community in which it is embedded. Liberals typically respond that they are committed to no such conception of the self: that the use they make of this is merely heuristic. And the debate rumbles on. This is a straightforward version of the dispute between lightness and weight. The dispute is this: in his or her self-understanding, how much lightness does a person contain – or can be realistically thought of as containing – and how much weight?

Each one of us is a combination of lightness and weight. That is the principal consequence of the Enlightenment. This is a good, not a bad, thing. The characteristic anxieties of modern moral and political thought turn on getting the balance right: just how much lightness and how much weight should the ideal person possess? And the characteristic problems that we face – both theoretical and practical – come when we don't, for one reason or another, get the balance right.

In particular, two sorts of breakdown in the modern self or person can occur. The first, straightforward, breakdown occurs when we fail to get the balance right between lightness and weight in our personalities. We then understand ourselves either as having no constitutive attachments to what we value or as being merely servants of those values. As we shall see, both of these forms of self-understanding can lead to problems. The second sort of breakdown is more serious and is built on the first. It stems from the fact that both objectivism and individualism have their degenerate forms: fundamentalism and relativism, respectively. The idea I want to explore in the next chapter is that the corresponding sort of degeneration can occur in the individual. Vfame, I shall argue, is a consequence of one form of this degeneration. The other consequence – the inverse of vfame – is somewhat more surprising.

5. From suicide bombers to Young Hot Hollywood

The fanatic and the ghost

Let us first consider a life of pure weight, unconstrained by the lightness of Enlightenment individualism. In its pure form, this is the life of the fanatic and slave. The life of weight is a life lived in service to values that transcend it, and in terms of which it is to be judged. As we have seen, the concept of individualism is made up of the ideas of autonomy and self-realization. The life of pure weight has no room for either of these ideas. The life one must choose is already determined by these objective and independent values. If one fails to reflect these values in one's thoughts and deeds, then one's life is, accordingly, deficient. You have not only failed your values, you have thereby also failed yourself. To the extent that such a life has any room for free choice or expression, this can occupy only the interstices of these values: the small, and therefore largely insignificant, areas of life in which these values hold no sway. In every major aspect of life, these objective and independent values specify both what you should think and what you should do, and to the extent you do not think or do what these values specify, both you and your life are inadequate.

We saw earlier how objectivism has its natural degenerate form: fundamentalism – objectivism without the argument or evidence. A corresponding degeneration will inevitably occur in a life of pure weight. A life lived in service to values is a life that ultimately becomes incapable of questioning those values. Accordingly, the values that this life reveres will stagnate. Since they are not refreshed by critical enquiry, since they are not constantly reinforced by the need to defend them through logic, argument and evidence, they will soon solidify into dead dogma. The life of pure weight soon becomes a dogmatic joke of a life.

The life of pure lightness, on the other hand, would be pitiful in a somewhat different way. The life of pure lightness is the life of individualism unconstrained by any belief in the idea of objective and independent values. With respect to such a life, the most important question we can ask is: what could give such a life any importance or significance? The life of pure lightness is a life of autonomy unconstrained by value. But, as we saw earlier, this means that autonomy unconstrained in this way undercuts the idea of self-realization. In the absence of objective and independent values there is nothing by which a person's life could be gauged or measured, and so no way of determining whether their self-realization has been a success or failure. In such a life, there is nothing that would count as success at realizing or developing oneself precisely because there is nothing that would count as failure.

There is a well-known myth of ancient Greece, sometimes used as a metaphor for a life like this (Camus 1955). Sisyphus was a mortal who had offended the gods in some way. Different versions of the myth tell different stories of just what this offence consisted in, but perhaps the most common account is that at some point after his death, Sisyphus persuaded the gods to let him return to earth temporarily, on an urgent errand of some sort. However, when he had returned to the land of the living, and felt the warmth of the sun on his face, he decided he didn't want to return to Hades, and so he stayed put. Ignoring numerous admonitions to return, he lived out many years in the light. Eventually, however, he was forcibly returned to Hades, and there was made ready his rock. His punishment was to roll a huge rock up a hill. When he reached the summit the rock would roll back down to the foot of the hill, and Sisyphus would have to begin his task all over again. And that, for Sisyphus, was pretty much it: for all eternity.

Accounts of this myth usually emphasize the arduous nature of Sisyphus's task. The boulder is usually recounted as huge, of a weight Sisyphus is barely capable of moving. Thus, every step on his journey to the summit taxes his heart, nerve and sinew to the utmost. However, I don't think the nastiness of Sisyphus's punishment can be understood in terms of the arduous character of his task. Suppose the gods had instead given him a small pebble, one that he might easily fit into his pocket. Sisyphus then takes a leisurely stroll to the summit. When he gets there, the pebble falls out, rolls to the foot of the hill, and Sisyphus must begin all over again. This, I think, scarcely mitigates the nastiness of Sisyphus's punishment (Taylor 1987). Nor does this nastiness lie in the fact that Sisyphus hates his task. Suppose the gods inculcated in Sisyphus a strange desire: to roll huge rocks up hills. So intense is this desire, that Sisyphus is never happy unless he is rolling rocks up hills. We can't really describe Sisyphus's fate as "punishment" any more. The gods have guaranteed him the eternal satisfaction of his most intense desire. They have, therefore, guaranteed him eternal happiness (*ibid.*). Nevertheless, his fate, it seems, is still a nasty one. Just because Sisyphus is happy rolling rocks up hill does not mean he *should* be happy doing this. He is so only because he is the dupe of the gods.

The real horror of Sisyphus's punishment lies neither in its difficulty nor in the fact that it is unpleasant. The nastiness of the punishment lies in its sheer futility. Whether Sisyphus reaches the top or not does not matter; when he does, the boulder will roll back down and he will be forced to begin all over again. Therefore there is nothing in Sisyphus's task that could count as success or failure. The gods might have availed themselves of many different variations on this theme: digging a hole and filling it in again; filling a bucket from a lake using a spoon while the water in the bucket leaks back into the lake; and so on. What underlies the nastiness of these sorts of punishments is their futility. The problem is not that one fails in these sorts of tasks; rather, it is that there is nothing in the tasks that could count as success.

The life of true lightness, a life unadulterated by any conception of objective value, is similar to Sisyphus's punishment in that there is nothing that could constitute success, because there is nothing that could count as failure. In this sort of life, all values come from within, as functions of one's choices. Therefore, whatever one chooses, one is automatically living up to the values embodied in those choices. There is nothing that could count as failure to live up to one's values, so there is nothing that could count as success in living up to one's values either.

In reflecting on the "mercy" of the gods, where they inculcate in Sisyphus an intense desire to roll boulders up hills, and thus guarantee him eternal fulfilment of his most intense desire, we can, I think, almost feel more sorry for Sisyphus in these circumstances than we do on the traditional version of the myth. At least, in the traditional telling, Sisyphus possesses some sort of dignity. Powerful but vicious beings have imposed his fate on him, and there is nothing he can do about it – not even die. But in his recognition of the futility of his labour, and in his contempt for the gods who have imposed this labour on him, Sisyphus at least possesses dignity. That is lost once the gods become merciful. Sisyphus now becomes little more than a deluded stooge. In this scenario we can, I think, legitimately claim that what makes Sisyphus happy should not make him happy. However, to say this presupposes that there is an objective system of value, a system of value that is independent of what Sisyphus actually chooses. For his actual choices are simply expressions of the happiness that has been induced in him by the gods' manipulations.

In a life that is truly light, there is no distinction between what makes us happy and what should make us happy. And there is no distinction here because there are no values that exist independently of our choices: values that we could use to draw this distinction. When our values are nothing more than a function of our choices, and have no existence independently of these, then our values are nothing more than expressions of us. They are our creations and, therefore, we dwarf them in the sense that they are asymmetrically dependent on us. We can make different choices and therefore endorse different values. But this does not, in a life that is light, change the identity of the persons we are. So we can exist without the particular values we endorse, but they cannot exist without us.

A life where one dwarfs what one values is the life of a ghost. There is nothing in this life that could give it enduring significance. A life can take on a grandeur that is proportional to the grandeur of the values with which the subject of the life – the person who lives the life – identifies. Precisely because the person dwarfs his values, there is nothing in his life that could give it objective and enduring value. The person can flit from one value to the next, never really being touched by the values he puts on and takes off like a coat, and never really being shaped by those values. There is nothing in this life that would count as success or failure. There are no standards which that life would have to meet and which might, in principle, give it meaning.

The suicide bomber

It is rare to find anyone who is entirely light or entirely heavy. Indeed, perhaps it is impossible to find anyone who is entirely light or heavy. To talk of a person as being light or heavy is not to provide some binary, all-or-nothing, evaluation of what they are. Rather it is to describe the relative balance of certain tendencies that they possess. There is a tendency, on the one hand, to understand oneself as the author and progenitor of one's values. And there is the counterbalancing tendency to understand oneself as constitutively attached to, and therefore defined in terms of, one's values. These tendencies are present in all of us. Each one of us has a tendency to understand himself or herself as light: floating free of any decisive connection to one's values. And each one of us also has a tendency to understand herself or himself as heavy: constituted, or indelibly shaped, by her or his values. The key is to get the balance right between these forms of self-understanding. And all the indications are that this is something that we are finding harder and harder to do.

Elements of both light and heavy forms of self-understanding can, in differing amounts, be found in each of us. This is because we are products of the West, a culture whose guiding principle is that each form of self-understanding, if taken in isolation, is bankrupt. Light and heavy forms of self-understanding are what philosophers sometimes call ideal types: abstractions that are rarely embodied in full and complete form in actual people. However, some people do approximate – get very close to being – these ideal types. Approximations to the heavy, fundamentalist, self are becoming more and more numerous and more chilling. Probably the closest approximation lies in the suicide bomber, and associated ilk.

It is no coincidence, I think, that more and more suicide bombers are "home grown". Nor is it any coincidence that many of them are recent converts to Islam. It is still less of a coincidence that many of these home-grown terrorists are former drug users or petty criminals. The sheer emptiness of those who have experienced the life of pure lightness – a life where one dwarfs what one values and so cannot anchor oneself by those values – makes them fertile soil for a purpose or cause, and, often, any purpose or cause will do. It is the desire to understand oneself as heavy – to find oneself anchored to one's values – that is the key. Which values serve as the anchor is often less important than the fact that they are heavy enough to provide that anchor. Therefore, the more vacuous one's life, the less meaning to be found in it, the more attractive objectivism – and its degenerate form, fundamentalism – becomes.

Central to the process that transforms someone into a terrorist or suicide bomber is the arduously but assiduously acquired ability to extinguish in himself or herself any spark of compassion or empathy for the victims: any spark of human kindness. This is not an easy thing to do. All humans, if they are not psychopaths or sociopaths, possess what Darwin (1871, 1872) called the "social sentiments". These are emotions such as sympathy, empathy and compassion. If, for example, you come across the scene of an accident and witness someone writhing in agony, then it is normal and natural to experience feelings of shock, horror, distress, empathy and compassion. This sort of emotional reaction to the scene comes as part of our natural biological heritage since they are, in part, what binds human societies together. All social mammals have these sorts of emotions to some extent; these are the mechanisms evolution hit on in order to guarantee social stability. To come across the scene and feel nothing would be abnormal. All things being equal, a negative reaction to suffering is normal, as is a positive reaction to joy.

In order to effectively carry out his mission, the terrorist must subvert his natural biological heritage. This is achieved by way of a rigorous process of conditioning aimed at inculcating in him the belief that the victims of his attack are not properly human. They do not count; they are outside the sphere of moral concern. At this time, religion in the form of Islam has been far and away the most successful at pursuing this strategy, combining the idea that the terrorist's victims are infidels, falling outside the body of Islam and therefore outside the scope of moral concern, with the promise of heavenly reward in the form of seventy-two virgins whose lot is, apparently, to eternally administer to the needs of the martyred. One of the defining qualities of the human animal is the ability to convince itself of pretty much anything. For obvious reasons, this strategy works best with the gullible and uneducated, with the less gullible and more educated typically pulling the strings. The collapse of objectivism into fundamentalism is far more easily achieved in people who are unable to recognize logical argument and unable to understand empirical refutation. However, the collapse is not restricted to the gullible and uneducated. Even ostensibly intelligent people can convince themselves of the absolute authority of their values over them. Thus, the attempted bombings of London night-clubs and the subsequent attempted suicide bombing of Glasgow airport in 2007 were both orchestrated and executed by qualified medical doctors.

Whatever the method employed to break the hold of the social sentiments, and whatever the ideology used to underwrite that effort, the result is the same. In the terrorist, what was most human has now become subservient to what is extra-human. The clearest indication of the humanity of the terrorist – in the form of natural feelings of empathy, sympathy and compassion – has been expunged and in its place we find the mission. But the mission is the result of, and an expression of, a certain value system. And that is what the terrorist, as weapon, becomes: he is merely a placeholder for his values. As a weapon, the terrorist is a human emptiness, a vacuum. The person has gone and in his place, sucked in by the emptiness, we find only his values. This is the ultimate expression of a life that is heavy, a life in which the person is constitutively attached to, and so defined in terms of, his values. The values that lay outside him – objectively and independently – have now come to possess him.

There are two ironies involved here; both are instructive and far from accidental. The first is that being the subject of training and conditioning regimes that have aimed to inculcate in him the belief that his victims are less than human, the terrorist has himself become less than a normal biological human. Or, rather, he has become extra-human. The necessity of this irony follows from the fact that the terrorist understands himself as constitutively attached to values that lie outside him. It is in our sympathy, empathy, compassion and fellow-feeling that we find the clearest expression both of our humanity – our natural biological humanity – and of the idea that other human beings are intrinsically valuable. You cannot lose one without losing the other. When you success-fully inculcate in someone the idea that other people are less than human, the person who remains is himself no longer a natural biological human, in the same way that a sociopath is not a natural biological human.

The second irony is that, in the process of forging himself into a weapon, the terrorist provides a particularly clear expression of the individualist ideal of self-realization. Consider the hours spent in the gym each day, and, perhaps, the difficult, arduous and dangerous trips to terrorist training caps in northwest Pakistan or surrounding regions. The terrorist is, in at least one clear sense, becoming all he can be; he is realizing himself to the limits of his capabilities. Again, this irony is not accidental, and follows from the analysis of the way in which self-realization presupposes an objective system of values that can be used to evaluate choices and actions. Individualism, properly understood, presupposes objectivism. And objectivism can so easily collapse into fundamentalism.

The suicide bomber is, then, a cautionary tale. It is an example of a life where all the lightness has been expunged, leaving only the heaviness of constitutive attachment to one's values. This is the life of the fanatic: a life where the balance between lightness and weight has been lost.

For the purposes of this book, however, it is the opposite type of imbalance that is important. This is a life unduly dominated by lightness, where the role of values that are objective and inde-pendent of the person who chooses and acts has been lost. It is to here that we must look in order to understand the rise of vfame. The terrorist, the suicide bomber: these are just one side of the coin. On the other, I shall argue, we find vfame and its various trappings.

Young Hot Hollywood

The rubric "Young Hot Hollywood" denotes a group of rich, young socialites living in the Hollywood Hills, including but not restricted to actors. Paris Hilton is one of the princesses of Young Hot Hollywood; so too is Lindsay Lohan. Lohan has been having a long on-off-again affair with a rehab centre in Utah. In fact, it's quite difficult to keep up with her. When I started writing this book, she had just gone back into rehab, about ten days after getting out of rehab. During those ten days she managed to squeeze in an episode of road rage, a car chase, an arrest for drunk driving and cocaine possession, another car crash and leaving the scene of an accident (she ran away on foot – allegedly). Then she went back to rehab. She came out for the Christmas break, and, at the time of writing, apparently was last seen spending the New Year in Europe swigging champagne out of a bottle. So, it wouldn't be altogether surprising if we find another stint in rehab looming on the horizon.

Many people profess to be disturbed by these sorts of antics. They like to see Lindsay Lohan as a cautionary tale of what can happen when fame and fortune is achieved at too tender an age. If only, they say, she could be more like Natalie Portman. I, too, find the antics disturbing, but for quite a different reason. The stars, we are sometimes told, are just like us. And of course they are just like us: who else would they be like? It's just that they do things with a little more panache. They can afford to do so.

They find themselves hanging out in the VIP section of Privé night-club, and almost certainly being paid for their time; we find ourselves sweatily crammed into the downmarket nightclub Pu-na-na after an hour in a queue trying to negotiate our way past some rather surly bouncers. They drink Crystal; we have to make do with Stella. Their clubs are populated by the beautiful people, with carefully manicured nails and hair and bodies hardened by hours spent daily with their personal trainer; in the Pu-na-na, our peers are flabby, drunken, and bellicose. These are beer-bellied men who think that a fight is the perfect way to cap off a night out, and women who think that the important thing when out on the town is to show some flesh, irrespective of the condition that flesh is actually in. These people have no conception of a manicure, and their hair is positively unkempt. It's all so deliciously Hogarthian. And, when we gratefully exit the Pu-na-na at closing time, the chances are that some or other terrorist may have put a bomb in the car parked across the street.

I exaggerate – a little. But my point is that if we can stereotype Young Hot Hollywood, then we can also do the same to the rest of us. And this realization, I think, leads to one, unambiguous, conclusion: if the stars are indeed just like us, then they are *better* versions of us. That's why I find the antics of Lindsay Lohan so disturbing. Lohan may well be a cautionary tale, but she's not the sort of tale we thought she was.

Whenever I hear of some new misadventure she has got herself into, I generally think one of two things. The first is: for God's sake get a taxi! You can afford it. The same advice also holds true for, off the top of my head, Paris Hilton, Nicole Ritchie and Mischa Barton. It also holds for Britney Spears whenever she has custody of her two boys, which, the way things are shaping up, sadly looks like being never. The second thought, however, is far more disturbing. The thought is that the princes and princesses of Young Hot Hollywood are simply killing time. They can find nothing to do with their lives, and so kill time through unnecessary profligacy, unnecessary car chases, unnecessary recreational drugs, unnecessary engagement to each other and so on. That, of course, is their choice. But their activities would mean nothing at all – certainly not to me – if we didn't recognize that there is a strong and persistent tendency in each one of us that compels us in the same way and propels us in the same direction.

The problem is that we're all Young Hot Hollywood, or at least we can be. It's just that most of us are less young, less hot and less

Hollywood. We are similarly afflicted by a life that is unduly light. We suffer from a life that is cut off, in all essential respects, from the existence of values in terms of which our choices might be gauged. Because of this, our lives become small and inconsequential. If our values are simply a matter of our choices, and have no objective validity independently of those choices, then we can endorse values or rescind our endorsement as we will. Our values, therefore, never truly touch us or shape us. They are a coat that we can put on and take off as we like. We shape the coat; the coat does not shape us. Similarly, our values, on this way of thinking about them, become expressions of us rather than we being expressions of them.

In a life with values like this, there can be no significance or grandeur. Grandeur does not come from the self. It comes from the world around us, and, most importantly, from the values that shape and structure that world. But in the absence of fundamental attachments to values outside us, any sense that we share common purpose and common fate with the world around us is lost. We busy ourselves with small things. We kill time and then we die.

The suicide bomber and Young Hot Hollywood, therefore, are tendencies that exist in all of us. They are also mirror images of each other. Yes, Paris Hilton is indeed the flipside of Osama bin Laden. More importantly, Paris Hilton and Osama bin Laden are just extreme versions of forms of self-understanding that exist in each one of us. The suicide bomber embodies one form of self-understanding: in this form, the self has become absorbed into the world. Through a process of psychological and ideological indoc-trination, the self becomes an emptiness that sucks in the values around it. Alternatively, although it amounts to the same thing, the self has melted away, trickled away into the values that now define it. The result is the life of a fanatic. In Young Hot Hollywood, on the other hand, the self has shrivelled away to a point. The self is a psychic atom, unshaped, and ultimately untouched, by the values that surround it. This is the life of a ghost.

In this chapter, the suicide bomber and Young Hot Hollywood have been used as symbols. Both are symbols of a certain sort of absence of balance. The life of the suicide bomber is one unduly weighed down by the presence of constitutive attachments to the world around it. The life of Young Hot Hollywood is a life that is unduly light, floating freely, in a pernicious and ultimately destructive way, of the values that might have given its life grandeur and purpose.

The challenge – and this was, in effect, the challenge that defined the Enlightenment and the resulting West – is to find a way of living a life that is both appropriately heavy and appropriately light. The recent rise and rise of vfame, I am now going to argue, is strong evidence for the belief that, in the West of the early twenty-first century, this challenge is not being met.

6. Paris Hilton and the end of history

Vfame and the decline of Enlightenment

Vfame exists because, in the early-twenty-first-century West, we are constitutionally incapable of distinguishing quality from bullshit. This book has tried to explain why we lost this ability. We lost our confidence in the possibility of values outside ourselves. Indeed, we could no longer even understand what sorts of things these might be. Therefore, we came to think it was all about us. And our lives – and we – became impoverished as a result.

Vfame is fame unconnected to quality; it is fame disconnected from objective value and objective standards of evaluation. Vfame is fame unconnected, in any important way, to the sorts of features – excellence, broadly construed – that traditionally made people famous. Thus, it is an example of the sort of levelling down of qualitative distinctions described and predicted by Kierkegaard. From the perspective of vfame, any way of being famous is just as good as any other. Vfame is the egalitarian version of fame: the new opium of the masses. There are no clear standards of quality that one must meet in order to be vfamous. With traditional fame, there were at least some standards. They were discipline specific, and they were not always adhered to in every case. But they were there at least in ideal form. There are no standards one must attain in order to acquire vfame, not even ideal standards. Vfame is not, in its essence, a matter of quality. Vfame has nothing to do with value.

So, the question is: under what sorts of circumstances could vfame become a prominent cultural phenomenon, indeed, arguably the most pronounced cultural phenomenon of our times? The answer is clear: in the circumstance that the general populace has abandoned its interest in quality. The more fundamental question is then: why would the general populace abandon its interest in quality? The reason, I have argued, consists in a peculiar form of degeneration that the Enlightenment can undergo. The essence of the Enlightenment was to see the key to human flourishing as lying in a combination of individualism and objectivism. The eighteenth century's newfound emphasis on individual choice as a key component of human welfare was to be combined with an older tradition of objective value that derived ultimately from Plato. However, this combination of Platonic quality and individual choice is unstable, and there are two types of degeneration that it might undergo.

The first is when Platonic objectivism degenerates into fundamentalism: objectivism without the evidence or argument. The second is when individualism degenerates into a vapid relativism that refuses to recognize distinctions of quality. The cultural rogue prion responsible for vfame is this latter sort of degeneration. Today, we find the Enlightenment assailed on both sides. On the one hand there is the religious fundamentalism of various stripes. There is the Christian fundamentalism that would, on the grounds of faith, entreat us to ignore one of the most empirically confirmed theories of all time – in terms of empirical confirmation, a theory that is on a par with the heliocentric theory of the solar system – and replace it with the teaching of a facile creationism. On the other hand, there is the Islamic fundamentalism that perpetrates spectacular atrocities. And scarcely a week seems to go by without some or other Islamic mob, numbering in the thousands, parading through the streets of some city or other calling for the death of someone or other: Jews, gays, "the West", cartoonists, award-winning novelists, teachers, teddy bears. These mobs provide as clear a vision as there gets of the subordination of the human to the extra-human.

Enlightenment, however, is under attack not only by fundamentalism, but also by the mirroring form of degeneration: the transformation of individualism into relativism. It is this degeneration that is responsible for the rise of vfame, and it provides, I think, a far more subtle threat. When Islamic countries talk of the "decadence" of the West, they are pointing, correctly, to this form of degeneration. The monstrous historical irony, of course, is that they fail to understand that their own way of life is founded on an opposing – mirroring – form of degeneration. The difference is that in the case of many Islamic countries this was never a *historical* degeneration; historically speaking, they were never properly subject to the Enlightenment. For the West, the degeneration is both ideological and historical.

Faced with both forms of degeneration – with the transformation of objectivism into fundamentalism and that of individualism into relativism – it is far from clear that the West, the West of the Enlightenment, the idea not the place, is going to survive.

The case of Joe Calzaghe

The inability to distinguish quality from bullshit is not just the lot of the masses; today it afflicts novices and experts alike. To paraphrase heavyweight boxing champion Joe Lewis, in the boxing ring you can run but you can't hide. You might think that the one-to-one gladiatorial combat of the ring is one place where vfame counts for nothing. Here, surely, it is only quality that counts; for quality is the only decisive factor determining the outcome of the bout. The quality of a fighter does not depend on what people believe; it is objective and independent of their beliefs, attitudes, opinions and hopes. The proof of quality is in the fighting, or so one might think.

But even here we find a puzzling, wilful and, above all, determined attempt to ignore quality as much as it is possible to do. If you doubt this, you need look no further than Joe Calzaghe.

Calzaghe became WBO super middleweight world champion in 1997 by beating Chris Eubank on points. Eubank was himself a very good former world champion. In beating him, Calzaghe also became the first person to knock Eubank off his feet in the ring. So, what did people say? Eubank was past it; Calzaghe beat only a pale imitation of the former Eubank. In fact, Eubank was only thirty-one, and these days that is relatively young for a boxer. Calzaghe is now thirty-six and, at the time of writing, is still an unbeaten, and indeed undisputed, world champion, indeed, the longest reigning world champion around.

Following his defeat of Eubank and assumption of the title of WBO super middleweight world champion, Calzaghe suffered from chronic hand and elbow damage caused, it was eventually discovered, by a glitch in his punching technique. Thus, at this time we find him limping to laboured victories over two former champions, Robin Reid and David Starie. Essentially, he beat both men – and both of them were still very capable fighters – with one hand tied behind his back (and that is not the only time he has won fights one-handed – ask Evans Ashira or Kabary Salem). But because he didn't demolish them in the spectacular manner his earlier fights had suggested he would, the consensus was that Calzaghe was either washed up or over-hyped or both.

The person who everyone assumed would take the title off this washed up/over-hyped no hoper was Omar Sheika. Sheika was widely touted as boxing's next big thing, and had for a couple of years been the terror of the Eastern United States. Everybody was predicting an easy win for Sheika. Calzaghe stopped him in five rounds. Bravo, Joe, one might think. However, this was not the general reaction. Instead, around this time, a common refrain started: Calzaghe has never fought anyone. Faced with a public unable to recognize quality, Calzaghe was becoming a victim of his own success. He was, in fact, so good at what he did that he was stopping anyone from becoming anyone. No one today really remembers Omar Sheika, but he was certainly going to be someone: indeed, in terms of boxing success, he already was, although people tended to forget that. By destroying him in such a one-sided fight, Calzaghe had permitted everyone to form the impression that Sheika was no one, and so grew the rather silly accusation that Calzaghe had never fought anyone.

There followed two very good fights with former world champions, and fighters: Byron "the Slama from Bama" Mitchell and the dangerous Charles Brewer. Increasingly desperate to put on spectacular performances and so gain the recognition that he felt, correctly, he wasn't being given, Calzaghe took unnecessary risks in both fights, risks that, given his consummate boxing skills, he really didn't need to take. Indeed, against Mitchell, Calzaghe had to get up off the canvas for the first time in his career. Nevertheless he won both fights convincingly.

Still, Calzaghe's success went on to haunt him. Years were spent chasing down the really big names in boxing – people such as Roy Jones Jr and Bernard Hopkins – but they didn't want any piece of him. Calzaghe was too good to risk fighting. And so, because the household names kept ducking him, the clamour continued to grow that Calzaghe hadn't really fought anyone. Eventually, however, when Calzaghe was thirty-four, there came what any reasonable person might have recognized as the acid test of his quality. Jeff "Left Hook" Lacy was a young world champion, touted as the future of boxing, the new Mike Tyson, someone who would save boxing from the new and serious challenge of the Ultimate Fighting Championship, or cage fighting. Few people gave Calzaghe any chance against Lacy: the fight was thought to be a formality for Lacy, his straightforward coronation as super middleweight champion. In fact, Calzaghe took him to school, and gave him a boxing lesson as one-sided as anything ever seen in a world championship fight. Not since the first Muhammad Ali–Cleveland Williams fight has there been boxing of such precision and perfection. Lacy was a young, strong and dangerous world champion – the saviour of boxing – and he didn't even win a round.

So, what conclusion did the boxing cognoscenti – the experts – draw from this? Did they conclude that Calzaghe was an exceptional fighter? There were, among some, the beginnings of a grudging acceptance that Calzaghe might be something special. But in general the mood was that Lacy had been over-hyped (they forgot to mention that this over-hyping was done by them). And as soon as the excitement generated by the fight had died down, people were once again singing their one note song: Calzaghe has never fought anyone. Yet again Calzaghe was the victim of his own success. Perhaps if the fight had been more even, if Lacy had managed to win some of the rounds, people might have had to reassess their verdict that he was over-hyped. But the fact that Calzaghe destroyed him in such a one-sided way ultimately counted against him. This was the pattern that had repeated itself throughout his career. Because he was such an exceptional fighter, because he was so much better than his peers, he created the impression – in minds that were, for reasons we shall discuss shortly, receptive to this thought anyway – that he had never fought anyone of any note. Some people ducked him; the rest he beat easily. Either way, Calzaghe loses.

Then, shortly before his thirty-sixth birthday, Calzaghe fought Mikkel Kessler. Kessler, a Dane, was (and is now again) a world champion and not just a good one, but an excellent one; indeed, he shows every sign that he will go on to become a great one. He is also eight years younger than Calzaghe: bigger, stronger and with a harder punch. Also, like Calzaghe, he was unbeaten. Calzaghe ran into some difficulties early on. He was fighting too square – too front on – and this was leaving him open to Kessler's formidable upper-cut. But with the sort of intelligence that has characterized his career, Calzaghe made adjustments: he started fighting more side-on, and won the fight – in the end, convincingly – through the use of his excellent southpaw right lead.

It was only now that people began to accept that Calzaghe might be something special. Ironically, his quality was finally established in the public's eye by what was, arguably, one of his worst performances: a split decision over Bernard Hopkins in Las Vegas. Moving up to light-heavyweight for the first time, Calzaghe looked a little slow and ponderous. But he was too busy for Hopkins, and won the fight by three or four rounds. You have to wonder what would have happened if Hopkins had been five years younger.

Ultimately, I think, Calzaghe made just one mistake: he was born too late. Calzaghe is an exceptional fighter: fast, skilful, intelligent, brave. But that's all he is. He could walk the walk, but he couldn't talk the talk: at least, he showed no interest in doing so. And that, in an age where vfame is doing its best to eclipse fame, an age where we are no longer able to distinguish quality from bullshit, just isn't enough. It's interesting, in this regard, to compare Calzaghe to someone who was coming up through the boxing ranks around the same time as him. During the mid-1990s, British boxing was dominated by "Prince" Naseem Hamed: a brash, flashy and distinctly unorthodox fighter from Sheffield. Hamed was a world champion, who relied on the power of his punch and the surprise generated by his unorthodox style. His fights were invariably entertaining. Hamed was ultimately unable to walk the walk, but he could talk the talk: at least, he thought he could and other people seemed to agree. In fact, talking the talk seemed to amount to outrageous ring entrances and a spiel that sounded like a poor man's Muhammad Ali: a theme of "I am the greatest", but performed without Ali's characteristic intelligence, wit and charm. Nonetheless, people bought it. Even the experts bought it. However, all the talk in the world couldn't help him when he ran into someone who was arguably his first world class opponent – the great Marco Antonio Barrera – and Hamed got taken apart.

In the UK at that time, Hamed was a household name, but outside of boxing few had heard of Calzaghe. The former was arrogant, mouthy and flashy, but in the end not very good. The latter was quiet and unassuming, but one of the best fighters there has ever been. Everything you need to know about the decline of Enlightenment can be found in the observation that Hamed was a household name and Calzaghe a relative unknown. This is an age that is defined by the inability – or at least the distinct unwilling- ness – to understand and recognize quality.

This, I emphasize again, is as true of experts as it is of novices. Boxing is a difficult, and subtle, art, and it would be one thing if the general population were unable to discriminate between an average and a great world champion. But this inability character- izes people who have spent their lives watching boxing, and, more importantly, have made their livings from their abilities to provide supposedly intelligent and informed opinions about the rela- tive merits of fighters. I'm talking about some boxing commen- tators who, despite a lifetime spent watching and thinking about boxing, may have slightly less ability to make fine discriminations of quality between boxers than has, for example, my wife, who hates the noble art. They would perhaps say that they are enti- tled to their opinions, and this is true. But this is the litany of the decline of Enlightenment. One may be entitled to one's opinion, but often your opinion should be better than it is. People who really know boxing – who know it because they've been there and done it – could recognize Calzaghe's quality. Sugar Ray Leonard could, and Emanuel Steward could. So too could Barry McGuigan. But the rest of the experts were unable to distinguish quality from bullshit. This is a symptom of an age where individ- ualism, and its degenerate form, relativism, have eclipsed objec- tivism about value. The inability, even of experts, to distinguish quality from bullshit is, in a nutshell, the consequence of the decline of Enlightenment.

Clusterfuck to the White House

The 2008 US Presidential election is now in full swing, and one thing is pretty clear: no one has any idea of how to evaluate the relative merits of the competing candidates. This was true all through the primaries, or, as *The Daily Show* more accurately put it, "the clusterfuck" to the White House. Many people hold out this election as a sort of beacon of hope shining out to the rest of the world. I, on the other hand, find it difficult to express just how depressing I find it all.

Let's review the story so far, beginning with the primaries. For the Democrats, the issues seemed to revolve around the following questions: is America ready for a woman President? Is America ready for a black President? And the crucial deciding factor, the only possible explanation for why the popular vote would go one way or another, was: which is the most prevalent in America, misogyny or racism? As the process went on, interesting sub-questions were thrown up from time to time. Is Obama black enough? Is Hillary human enough? And can America really vote for someone whose parents were myopic enough to call Barack Hussein (as in Saddam) Obama (rhymes with Osama).

Accompanying all this was much hand-wringing about the role of the press. Indeed, it was fairly typical to blame the press. They insisted on presenting the relative merits of each candidate as a weighted combination of the following: being likeable, looking presidential, whether someone is black enough, whether someone is too black, whether someone is too white; even whether someone is sufficiently human. They stopped just short of ranking presidential candidates according to how hot their spouses are (if they had, the money would have been on Dennis Cucinich). Now, while I'm inclined to agree that the press are rarely blameless – for anything – it is difficult to see how they could get away with the trivialization of a contest the importance of which, after eight years of George W. Bush, everyone in the world recognizes, unless the general population were, in some way, receptive to this trivialization. The proliferation of news channels in recent years has left all of them desperate for viewers, and they are going to go with what people want, on some level, to see.

For the Republicans, the spectacle was even more unedifying. Three of the leading Republican candidates professed not to believe the theory of evolution, thus demonstrating that they had failed to achieve even minimal levels of educational attainment. If they had been in my school they would have been put in the "slow" class. The eventual nominee was John McCain. Since then, even serious news programmes have been running with the following, appalling, sub-text: John McCain is old. No, I mean, John McCain is really old. Apparently, ageism is far more prevalent in America than sexism or racism.

The lack of clear policy on the part of either candidate is, admittedly, depressing. This lack is, perhaps, not just their fault. As soon as they try to say, clearly, what their policies are, the other side jumps on them, and quickly twists them into an unrecognizable parody. But what's most depressing is that this doesn't seem to matter. People would apparently much prefer to hear a parody of the views of the person to which they have antecedently taken a dislike than hear what their views really are. It seems that the average voter has already decided who they are going to vote for, and all they want to now hear is evidence that confirms their choice, whether true or not. For all the demonizing of Bush, that's all he did with the invasion of Iraq.

Throughout all this, it's not that people had a list of criteria that they would like to be met, and were simply not sure which candidates, if any, were going to meet them. Judgements of this sort are often difficult to make, and a failure of this sort would be understandable. Indeed, it would be almost comforting. But the failure was far more disturbing. Apparently, the voting population didn't, in general, have any list of criteria that it would like to see met. Knowing how to make a judgement – knowing what criteria to use – but being unable to make it in particular cases is one thing. But not knowing how to make the judgement at all is a far more serious kind of failure. In this case, not only are you unable to make a good judgement – unless it's by accident – but, far worse, you have no idea what would even constitute a good judgement. Our lives have become so light, the influence of Platonic objectivism on us has become so attenuated, that we have lost our grip on the idea that there can be objective standards of evaluation that transcend our likes and dislikes. We have lost track of the idea that anything could be more important than our affections.

A theory of quality

The principal symptom of the degeneration of individualism into relativism is an unwillingness, and eventually an inability, to adjudicate on issues of quality. We are no longer able to distinguish quality from bullshit because we have lost any grip on the idea that there might be objective standards of evaluation even for some of the most important choices we can make. Issues of quality are issues of value, and in the transformation of individualism into relativism, these issues have been rendered marginal. First we became unconcerned with the quality of the people we elect to lead us. Eventually, we even forget what quality is: we forget even how to think about the issue of quality. Thus, we transform our political leaders into Naseem Hameds: talkers of the talk but not walkers of the walk. In the most important decisions we can make, we have not only lost sight of what is important, we have lost the ability to even think about what makes something important. So, how should we think of quality?

Basically, I don't know. I am a product of the Enlightenment just like everyone else I know. I don't know how to think about quality: about what it really is. The best I can do is try to identify a *criterion* of quality: an account that tells us when something has quality, and that allows us to make judgements of relative quality, but that falls far short of telling us what quality really is. It is a measure of how far I am from really understanding quality that the criterion I am going to propose is a *quantitative* one.

Quality is, of course, discipline specific. What makes for quality in a boxer is not what makes for quality in a political leader. But is there any more general way of thinking about quality, one that abstracts from the details of the discipline under consideration? I think there probably is. And here, in a tentative, provisional way, I want to sketch some of the outlines of a way of thinking about a criterion of quality in general.

Marx famously defended a labour theory of value. According to this theory, the value of an object or commodity is a function of the labour that had to be put in to producing it. This theory of value fell apart under the inconvenient observation, made by people such as twentieth-century economist Ludwig von Mises, that, in fact, things were worth whatever people were willing to pay for them. Thus, if socialist systems were based on the labour theory of value, there would be no realistic way of fixing prices in them; in practice such price-fixing would occur by piggybacking on prices in surrounding non-socialist systems. Therefore, predicted von Mises back in 1922, socialist economic systems would eventually collapse, which, of course, they did.

The alternative capitalist approach, in essence, sees economic value as a function of supply and demand, rather than labour. It doesn't matter how many days, months or even years of labour you have put into producing a given item, if there are many of those items around anyway, or if people have no interest in them, then it's not going to be worth very much. Economic value depends essentially on supply and demand; relative scarcity or rarity is a value-conferring property.

The criterion of quality I am going to develop draws on elements of both Marxist and capitalist conceptions of value. From Marxism, I am going to borrow the idea that quality of a skill or talent depends on the amount of work that needs to be put into acquiring that level of skill or talent. From capitalism, I am going to borrow the idea that quality of a skill or talent is a function of relative rarity or scarcity.

Suppose someone says, as I'm sure someone, somewhere, has:

Britney is just as good as Beethoven.

Interestingly enough, I once had a colleague who believe something pretty much like that. For her, quality is just a social construction, although in her defence, she was a sociologist and sociologists like to think that everything is a social construction. To the extent that things are not social constructions, they do not form part of the subject matter of sociology. And if enough things are not social constructions, sociologists are out of a job. However, quality is not, in fact, a social construction, and the idea that it is is just another symptom of the degeneration of individualism into relativism.

Why might someone, even an intelligent person, be tempted to think that Britney Spears is just as good as Ludwig van Beethoven? The easiest, most straightforward, route is based on the idea that there are no objective standards of evaluation in terms of which the relative merits of Spears and Beethoven could be assessed. Spears does her thing, Beethoven does – or rather did – his, and that's all you can say. It's apples and oranges or, sticking with flora, let a thousand flowers bloom and so on.

This is, I think, truly facile. But before I explain why, I should say a few words about poor old Britney Spears. I'm not, in any way, Britney bashing. There's far too much of that going on anyway, and I certainly don't want to join in. She's not my cup of tea – my musical tastes run from Mozart to Metallica, but they do stop on the way to encompass pop – but Spears is apparently very good at what she does. Moreover, when you look at the massive corpus of her work, it is impossible not to be impressed with the sheer hard work she has put into it. In many respects she is – or, rather, was until recently – the epitome of the Enlightenment ideal of self-realization: of being all you can be. And more than that, what's easily lost in dwelling on the human train wreck that her life has become is the rather sweet teenager from Kentwood, Louisiana who would, in deference to her Baptist upbringing, always say "Oh my gosh" instead of "Oh my God". Nevertheless, to claim that Spears is just as good as Beethoven is ridiculous. And here's why.

The quality of Beethoven is a function of two things. First of all – and here is the Marxist element of the analysis – there is the amount of work you would have to put in to being Beethoven, or to writing music with an equivalent level of complexity, subtlety and power. When I was a child my mother, who had high if rather misguided hopes for me, used to lock me in the sitting room for an hour every day to make me practise the piano; since I was a rather wilful child, the lock was entirely necessary. Without any sort of exaggeration, I can confidently say she would have had more luck trying to turn me into a female pop icon. Indeed, I, now a muscular and hairy man in my forties, would still have more chance of being Britney Spears than Ludwig van Beethoven. The sex change, the hormones, the weight loss, the singing lessons: all this would be easier than trying to write something that even approximated the towering, cascading, crescendos of the third movement of the Emperor Concerto.

Secondly – and here is the capitalist element of the analysis – we must also consider just how many people could be Beethoven versus how many could be Spears. Spears is an OK singer: I'll grant you that. Someone might even say that she's a good singer: and, for the sake of argument, I'll grant you that too. But how many people can sing as well as Spears? The answer is, of course, many; at the very least, in a population of nearly seven billion, the answer has to run into millions, or hundreds of millions. Spears can dance. But how many can dance as well as she can? The answer is similar. Spears sings good songs, you might want to claim. But, of course, she doesn't write them; professional writers do. And how many of them are there: how many that could write songs of similar levels of quality? The answer is a straightforward empirical fact: tens or even hundreds of thousands. But how many people can write what Beethoven wrote: the third movement of the Fifth Piano Concerto, the final movement of the Ninth Symphony, the first movement of the Sixth Symphony, the first movement of the Fifth Symphony? The answer is not many, if any.

This claim is not intended as an advertisement for the merits of classical music over pop. We could use this account of quality to compare Spears, again unfavourably, to one of her peers, Christina Aguilera. Aguilera is an objectively better singer in at least one respect because she has a skill that Britney does not. Aguilera can hit a high E: the E that is two octaves above middle C. Spears can't do this, and, indeed, very few people can (Mariah Carey and Whitney Houston are two who can, but there are not many more). If we assume, for the sake of argument, that all other things are equal with regard to their singing quality, then on the account of quality developed here, Aguilera's singing is of higher quality than Spears's on general grounds of the rarity of her talent.

The quality of a person's talents – the sort of thing fame used to track but has recently abandoned – is a function of labour and rarity. The two are connected. Rarity pertains largely – although not exclusively – to the innate abilities of the person. There are few people born with the ability to write what Beethoven wrote, or to write what Tolstoy wrote, or to think what Aristotle, Kant or Einstein thought. There are few people born with the ability to hit the high E. Labour pertains largely to what must be put in to developing those innate talents to produce the work of towering genius that these people in fact produced. This includes not just the sheer slog, or effort, involved, but also the ability to not only withstand suffering or adversity but to draw from it and grow because of it. It would be misleading to suppose that these are entirely distinct things; the ability to slog, day in day out, and to draw strength and creativity from suffering are innate talents too. Ultimately, we cannot decipher just how much of the quality of a talent derives from innate factors and how much from environmental ones. Nonetheless, this does not stop us claiming that the quality of a talent is a function of its rarity and the amount of work that had to be put in to developing it.

Quality – the quality of a talent or ability – is a function of rarity and labour. The quality of Stanley Matthews – and the quality of a David Beckham judged purely as a footballer – is a function of just how many people there are who could emulate their skills and achievements, and, assuming they had the requisite natural talent, just how hard they would have to work in order to do so. The same is true of quality of any sort of talent. I have argued that fame, in the traditional sense, was associated with respect. And it was associated with respect because it tracked excellence or quality. We now see, at least roughly, what a quantitative criterion of quality would look like. The value of any quality is a function of how long would it take for me to acquire that quality. It is a function of how hard I would have to work to acquire it. And it is a function of how many people have the innate natural talents necessary to make that long and hard work pay off.

Letters from Lynwood jail

The degeneration of individualism into relativism consists in the unwillingness – and eventually the inability – to accept that there are distinctions of quality between the lives people choose to lead or the way in which they realize themselves: one way is just as good as any other. One manifestation of this, I have argued, is the rise of vfame: the inability to acknowledge distinctions of quality in the lives people choose to lead goes hand in hand with the inability to recognize distinctions of quality in the talents they possess. So vfame, I have argued, is a symptom of this more general degeneration of individualism into relativism. But what if someone were to embrace relativism, and issue the following challenge: OK – so what if we refuse to understand quality or recognize distinctions of quality? So what if we can no longer distinguish quality from bullshit? What reason is there for thinking that we are in any way worse off because of this inability? Maybe we're happier this way.

The correct response is that quality and bullshit don't care about whether we acknowledge them or not. They are there – and they are going to have the ramifications they have – irrespective of whether we recognize them. The most obvious consequence of the inability to distinguish quality from bullshit is that we make poor choices; we opt for bullshit when what our lives really needed at that time was a little bit of quality.

Ultimately, the most deleterious consequence of the inability to distinguish quality and bullshit is that it leaves us ill equipped to think about our own lives and so make them better. I was given a rather forceful reminder of this recently by the plight of a friend of mine. Let us call him Wayne. Wayne is a young philosophy instructor, working in a different university from me. His noble attempt – not to mention professional obligation – to acquaint his students with the wonders of the philosophy of religion had an unfortunate result. One of the students complained to Wayne's

Dean on the grounds that his personal religious beliefs were being violated. His personal beliefs, the student claimed, are sacrosanct and immune to criticism. By this the student did not mean that his personal religious beliefs are immune to criticism in the sense that all criticism is necessarily epistemically untenable. On the contrary, the student might acknowledge that the problem of evil, and the failure of the standard theodicies, do pose certain epistemic problems for his belief in an omnipotent, omniscient and omnibenevolent deity. What the student meant is not that his beliefs *can not* be criticized. He meant that they *should not* be criticized. Criticism of his personal religious beliefs is, the student maintained, morally wrong. Unfortunately for Wayne, his institution is an unenlightened one, and the Dean ordered Wayne to stop teaching philosophy of religion.

The student's way of life is grounded in his beliefs. Since his way of life is sacrosanct, so too are his beliefs. However, his beliefs are ungrounded in logic or evidence, where these provide certain standards that a belief must meet in order to be regarded as legitimate. Therefore, concluded the student (and the Dean), so much the worse for logic and evidence; so much the worse for objective standards of validity.

The case of Wayne reveals the deep – and in this book largely unexplored – connection between relativism and fundamentalism. The student is a fundamentalist, but has used a relativist strategy to "defend" his beliefs; what is personal is immune to criticism. Relativism can, and often is, used as a way of denying the legitimacy of the requirement of logic and evidence with regard to a particular domain of enquiry. However, as we have also seen, what occasions the degeneration of objectivism into fundamentalism is the abandonment of the legitimacy of logic, argument and evidence. On one level, relativism and fundamentalism are opposed; the fundamentalist preacher of whatever religion will have no time for the plea to let a thousand flowers bloom. However, on a deeper level, relativism and fundamentalism are connected as mutually supporting parts of the same process, or *dialectic* as philosophers sometimes call it.

For our purposes, however, what is important is another question: what does the fundamentalist student lose when he insists in wrapping his beliefs in cotton wool? By facing the criticisms of his belief, by acknowledging their apparent force, he is then forced to look at his beliefs with a view to defending them from these criticisms. In the process, he might further refine his beliefs, identifying, and where possible removing, their weaknesses and building on their strengths. His beliefs thereby become better than they were before. Not only that: he understands them better than he did before, and so becomes more comfortable with them. The beliefs become, more completely, his own rather than something alien that has been imposed on him. These possibilities are, of course, what fundamentalism, with its insistence on the inviolability of beliefs, precludes. You cannot make your beliefs better than they are, for they are already perfect. And for this reason, when you are a fundamentalist your beliefs never really become your own; they always stand over and above you, as irreducibly alien.

This inability to hone your logical and evidential skills in this most important arena of your personal beliefs leaves you, ultimately, ill equipped to deal with life. It leaves you ill equipped to think about the most important things in life such as what a good life is, and how is the best way to live it. And this, finally, brings us back to Paris Hilton, and her post-release interview with Larry King.

King: Let's hear some of the things you – what did you write in prison, in jail?
Hilton: Well, I had a lot of time alone, so I would write a lot. I actually have a journal with all the – I left it at home.
King: You kept a daily journal?
Hilton: Yes, I did. OK. This is one of the notes that I wrote. "They say when you reach a crossroad or a turning point in life, it

really doesn't matter how we got there, but it's what we do next after we got there. Usually you arrive there by adversity, and then it is then and only then that we find out who we truly are and what we're truly made of. It's a process, a gift and a journey, and if we can travel it alone, although the road may be rough at the beginning, you find an ability to walk it. A way to start fresh again. It's neither a downfall nor a failure, but a new beginning."

And I feel like this is a new beginning for me, to see jail – and I just used it as a journey to figure out myself and who I am and what I want to do. And there's just so much more to me than what people think.

Since she left her journal at home, but has brought this particular entry with her, one might surmise that this is an epistle of which she is particularly proud. But what it turns out to be is a rather clichéd crossroads narrative of the sort that a hormonal twelve-year-old might easily produce. When individualism degenerates into relativism, and we have no logical or rational acumen on which to fall back, all we can come up with are clichés. The decline of the Enlightenment is the transformation of life into kitsch (Kundera 1973). I'm sure Hiltons's journal entry is heartfelt – at least it was when she wrote it. But a sure sign of the decline of Enlightenment is the idea that heartfelt is good enough.

OK, I know, I'm just another sneering academic. But I'm not sneering at Hilton. I actually rather admire her, and what she's managed to achieve with what she's got. I'm sneering at us. We have become incapable of thinking about ourselves in any other terms than cliché. Whenever I see or hear a journalist asking a parent whose son or daughter has been killed in Iraq or Afghanistan how they feel, and thinking that this says anything relevant about whether we should be there, I see the decline of Enlightenment. To the extent that we are able to think about ourselves and what we should be doing with our lives, we can do so only in terms that are irrevocably kitsch. And everything else, all the other facets of ourselves that we are no longer capable of critically examining, we leave to an orgy of feelings. That our principal access to ourselves today is through our feelings is the sign of the collapse of Enlightenment.

Hilton tells us that she used her time in jail "as a journey to figure out myself and who I am and what I want to do". This might lead us to think that she learned something valuable during the twenty-two days she spent at Lynwood. Certainly, King took this to be an implication of what she said:

King: Do you think you've found yourself?

Hilton: I feel like I've started my journey and I'm going to continue every day to find out more and more about myself.

King: What don't you like about Paris Hilton? What's a personality trait Paris Hilton would change?

Hilton: Something – when I get nervous or shy, my voice gets really high. I've been doing that ever since I was a little girl. And that's something that I don't like that I do. I like it when I talk in my normal voice, but sometimes I go down, and that's something I'm trying to change about myself.

King: Are you jealous?

Hilton: No.

King: Quick to anger?

Hilton: No, I don't really get angry.

King: Easy to get along with?

Hilton: I'm very easy to get along with.

King: Good friend?

Hilton: A very loyal friend.

Hilton did say that it was only the start of her journey. But, by her account it seems she doesn't have very far to go. I wish I were as perfect as Paris: no jealousy, no anger, easy to get along with and a loyal friend. In fact, the only respect she can identify in which she falls short of perfection is that her voice gets high and squeaky when she's nervous. That's what she learned about herself from her stay in Lynwood: she doesn't like the way her voice gets when she's nervous. Is there anyone who has ever learned more about themselves from time spent incarcerated? Eat your heart out, Alexander Solzhenitsyn.

This is, of course, unfair. There is no reason to suppose that ex-cons should necessarily know more about themselves than those never incarcerated. But, again, I should emphasize that I'm not laughing at Hilton, I'm laughing at us. We are the people who routinely pay her several hundred thousand pounds merely to show up at a nightclub. We are the people who buy clothes from her fashion line or perfume from her perfume line. We are the people whose news programmes devote a large portion of a day to her being sent back to Lynwood jail. If it is so easy to make jokes at Hilton's expense, then the joke must surely be on us.

This is the culmination of the decline of Enlightenment, and a resulting life of lightness. We become unable to think about ourselves, unable to understand ourselves, in any other terms than clichés. We vaguely hear things from somewhere or other – the kitsch magazines we read, the kitsch television programmes we watch – and then not only do we pass them off as our own views, but we even come to understand ourselves in these terms – terms that are invariably derivative and trite.

The culmination of the decline of Enlightenment is to lose track of who you are. To understand ourselves, we have to anchor ourselves by our values, and by objective standards of quality, that exist independently of us. But the values that existed outside us have withered away, and we follow quickly on their heels.

The end of Enlightenment?

Each one of us is a composite of individualist and fundamentalist. Individualism and fundamentalism are different and competing forms of self-understanding. We mirror the culture that made us; we are fractured creatures whose being must be continually achieved by way of a delicate balancing act that requires skill, understanding, fortitude and more than a little dissembling. This balancing act is not something that can be achieved indefinitely, and this is true both at the level of the individual and the culture that he or she embodies.

The existence of vfame is evidence of a culture whose individualism has lost its objectivist counterbalance, and as a result is constantly buffeted between a facile form of relativism and a chilling form of fundamentalism. In this culture, each way of developing yourself as a person is just as legitimate and valuable as any other. Therefore, it doesn't matter why you are famous, just that you are. And having no independent and objective values with which to measure our lives, we think that validation is to be found in the simple – and largely baseless – recognition of our peers. The result is vfame.

Political economist Francis Fukuyama, following nineteenth-century philosopher G. W. F. Hegel, once talked of the end of history (1993), and speculated that in modern liberal democracy history had in fact come to an end: a mistake that, given subsequent events, is difficult to live down. (Hegel, on the other hand, thought that history came to an end when he put the last full stop to the last sentence of *Phenomenology of Spirit*: an event that coincided with the world spirit, instantiated in Hegel, achieving awareness of itself). Embodied in such an idea is a conception of history as progressive, leading to more and more perfect forms of society until some stable, and perfect, end point is reached. I doubt that history is progressive in this way.

Far more plausible, and worrying, is the idea that the en-vehicling of Paris Hilton – or, rather, our ridiculous fascination with it – signals something like the end of Enlightenment. History, I suspect, is sporadic rather than progressive. Every now and then it produces exceptional eras or epochs, populated by exceptional people: people who are allowed to be exceptional by the epoch itself. But such epochs have their inevitable by-products, produced in their process of self-initiated decline. It is not so much Young Hot Hollywood or a plethora of reality television shows, but our risible fascination with these things and what they represent, that provides the most graphic example of this decline. Spectacular eruptions of history of the sort that produced the Enlightenment also produced Paris Hilton. And I have tried to show why there is more than an accidental connection between the two.

The fundamentalist backlash has, of course, already begun: in various forms; from the Islamic fascism that perpetrates spectacular atrocities, to the rise of the Christian right that wants to see the teaching of evolution banned in schools. This is just the other side of the coin. Enlightenment, being composed of two ideas, can decline on two fronts. The end of Enlightenment is heralded by a plethora of princes and princesses of Young Hot Hollywood. It is heralded by our fascination with these. And for every one of these, as part of the same underlying historical necessity, there is an Osama bin Laden.

I feel privileged, and very lucky, to have been born during the age of Enlightenment. An age like this is not to be judged on how long it lasts, but on how brightly it burns. We enjoy it while we can. But vfame, and the fundamentalism that mirrors it, are, I suspect, signs that the candle is burning out.

Further reading

Adorno and Horkheimer's *Dialectic of Enlightenment* (1973), first published in Germany in the immediate post-war era, is the classic study of the perils and pitfalls of the Enlightenment, and introduces the idea of the "dark side" of Enlightenment, of which the holocaust was one expression. Charles Taylor has done more than anyone to put into question the concept of the self implicated in the Enlightenment; and the associated ideal of self-realization. See his *Sources of the Self* (1984), and its somewhat breezier little brother, *The Ethics of Ambiguity* (1992). A similar sort of critique has been developed by Charles Guignon in his *On Being Authentic* (2004).

In literature, the work of Milan Kundera positively resonates with the sorts of themes discussed in this book. His most famous work is *The Unbearable Lightness of Being* (1973). But see also The *Book of Laughter and Forgetting* (1982), *Laughable Loves* (1975) and pretty much anything he has ever written.

References

Adorno, T. & M. Horkheimer 1973. *Dialectic of Enlightenment*. New York: Continuum.

Camus, A. 1955. *The Myth of Sisyphus*, Justin O'Brien (trans.). Harmondsworth: Penguin. First published in French as *Le Mythe de Sisyphe* (Paris: Gallimard, 1942).

Darwin, C. 1871. *The Descent of Man and Selection in Relation to Sex*. London: John Murray.

Darwin, C. 1872. *The Expression of the Emotions in Man and Animal*. London: John Murray.

Fukuyama, F. 1993. *The End of History and the Last Man*. New York: Harper Perennial.

Guignon, C. 2004. *On Being Authentic*. London: Routledge.

Hegel, G. W. F. 1977. *Phenomenology of Spirit*, A. Miller (trans.). Oxford: Clarendon Press.

Kierkegaard, S. 1962. *The Present Age*. New York: Harper & Row.

Kundera, M. 1973. *The Unbearable Lightness of Being*. London: Faber.

Kundera, M. 1975. *Laughable Loves*. Harmondsworth: Penguin.

Kundera, M. 1982. *The Book of Laughter and Forgetting*. London: Faber.

Nietzsche, F. 1969. *Thus Spoke Zarathustra: A Book for All and None*, R. J. Hollingdale (trans.). Harmondsworth: Penguin.

Sartre, J.-P. 1947. *Situations I*. Paris: Gallimard.

Sartre, J.-P. 1958. *Being and Nothingness*, Hazel Barnes (trans.). London: Methuen. First published in French as *L'Être at le Néant* (Paris: Gallimard, 1943).

Taylor, C. 1984. *Sources of the Self*. Cambridge: Cambridge University Press.

Taylor, C. 1992. *The Ethics of Authenticity*. Cambridge, MA: Harvard University Press.

Taylor, R. 1987. "Time and Life's Meaning". *Review of Metaphysics* **40**: 675–86.

Von Mises, L. 1951. *Socialism: An Economic and Sociological Analysis*. New Haven, CT: Yale University Press.

Index